CHARLES I
AT THE TIME OF HIS TRIAL

THE TRIAL OF
CHARLES I

A contemporary account taken from the memoirs of
Sir Thomas Herbert and John Rushworth
Edited by Roger Lockyer

Roger Lockyer

INTRODUCTION BY C. V. WEDGWOOD

FOLIO PRESS: J. M. DENT
LONDON 1974

Distributed for the Folio Press
202 Great Suffolk Street, London SE1 by
J. M. DENT & SONS LTD
Aldine House, Albemarle Street, London W1

Folio Society first edition of 1959,
with letterpress text and gravure illustrations,
reprinted by photo-litho in 1974

ISBN 0 460 04156 8

PRINTED IN GREAT BRITAIN
by Whitstable Litho, Whitstable
Set in Baskerville type
Bound by J. M. Dent & Sons Ltd, Letchworth

CONTENTS

ILLUSTRATIONS

INTRODUCTION

THE formal trial and public execution of a King by his
own subjects was an event unprecedented in the history
of European nations when King Charles I was arraigned,
condemned and beheaded in January 1649.

The startled clamour which the event provoked from the
governments of Western Europe died down with surprising
speed as the republican government established itself in
England, and statesmen who had expressed abhorrence at
the murder were within a few years on easy political terms
with the murderers. The pressing needs of international
policy account for this slurring over of the event, but the
moral and political significance of the King's death was to
grow larger, not smaller, in the lengthening perspective of
history. This was in great part the effect of the King's own
conduct; as the details became known and appreciated he
was seen to have gone towards his doom with extraordinary
firmness of purpose and to have revealed in his last ordeal
an unshaken spirit that compelled respect both for him and
for his cause.

King Charles differed in character and in conduct from
the two other monarchs who, in the French and the Russian
Revolutions, succumbed to sentences passed on them by so-
called tribunals of the people. King Louis XVI and Tsar
Nicholas II were victims of circumstances over which they
had little control. King Charles was directly responsible for
the position in which he found himself. To state this is not

in any way to disparage the King; it is no disparagement of the early saints and witnesses of the Christian religion to say that they brought their martyrdom on themselves by declaring their faith. The King held certain views about the nature of Christian monarchy which made it a matter of conscience for him to act as he did. He deliberately tried to eradicate other, and as he thought, pernicious views. By so doing he cut across the interests of many of his subjects and united against him the opposition which overthrew and destroyed him. It is not necessary to agree with the King's opinions to accord him the right to the name of martyr. Still less is it necessary to approve the mistaken methods which he often employed to gain his ends. His integrity lay not in his political conduct but in the unshaken constancy with which he held to his own conception of kingship. He believed himself to be called by the grace of God, operating through his unquestioned hereditary right, to rule over his people for their good. He believed that he could not abandon certain essential prerogatives of the Crown without committing a grave sin, against his successors on the throne, against the people who had been entrusted to his care, and above all against God who had ordained his sovereignty. Because he would not abandon this belief and these rights he died, and for no other reason.

King Charles had no premonition of martyrdom during his earlier and outwardly prosperous years. No fate seemed less likely to be his. Although a few perceptive foreign envoys noticed the unrest in the country and predicted storms ahead of him, he did not anticipate them himself. At the height of his power in 1637 he described himself as "the happiest King in Christendom".

But he had from the first, in good fortune and in bad, the singleness of mind which is often the foundation of the martyr's temperament. As a young man he said once in a light-hearted discussion with friends that he would never have made a lawyer for he could not 'defend a bad nor yield in a good cause.' This was a significant statement and foreshadowed the obstinacy which he was later to show in defence of the royal prerogative.

At his Coronation he made an important modification to his oath, swearing to respect the liberties of the people only in so far as they did not clash with the prerogative of the Crown. He believed that, in the last resort, God had made him sole judge of the rights and interests of his subjects. It was by no means an ignoble belief. The text for the sermon preached at his Coronation, a text which he must surely have approved, was 'Be thou faithful unto death and I will give thee a Crown of life.' Nothing could have better expressed his belief that the whole of his mortal life was dedicated to the right exercise of his kingly office.

Again, in the first winter of the Civil War when the King still had every reason to expect a rapid victory, he wrote in a private letter that he meant to be either 'a glorious King or a patient martyr'. This was a clear statement that he would admit neither surrender nor compromise as a way out of the war; either he would have a complete victory or he would fight to the last whatever the consequences sooner than abandon what he believed to be his sacred duty.

This intransigence of the King, an intransigence springing from what was essentially a religious conception of his office, was the most important single factor in bringing him to his tragic end. It had been clear before Queen Elizabeth I died that a struggle for power between the monarch and Parliament could not long be postponed. All over Europe during this century of decision monarchs sought to strengthen and centralize their power in order to create efficient modern states. The cumbrous local and representative institutions which had grown up during the middle ages were being challenged and destroyed. But a few of these institutions, of which the English Parliament was one, had as much resilience and modernity as the sovereign, and had moreover a dangerous power over him because they were the principal source through which he obtained money. Elizabeth, by dexterous management of her Parliaments and by a subtle judgment of popular reactions, had successfully maintained the authority of the Crown. King James I never had the old Queen's infallible popular touch, and in the course of his reign he gradually allowed Elizabeth's clever custom of managing Parliament through court officials, whose task it was to organize the presentation of the royal policy to their fellow members—government spokesmen, as we should say—to fall into disuse.

When King Charles ascended the throne in March 1625 it was clear that the repeated deadlocks between King and Parliament could not continue for much longer. One or other would have to find means to prevail. As the situation stood the King's policy was constantly blocked by Parliament's refusal to vote supplies, but Parliament had not yet gained the power to initiate policy itself, still less the power to force its wishes on the King. The King stood for the authoritarian solution of this problem by freeing himself from financial dependence on Parliament and reducing it to the position of an advisory council. Parliament, or rather its more dynamic leaders, stood for a solution by which they would themselves gain a say in the nomination of the King's councillors and the framing of his policy. Both parties believed that their point of view was justified by the ancient law and practice of England and both were wrong. King and Parliament were in fact facing a new situation brought about by the social and economic changes of the last century, which neither of them fully understood.

No man called to the government of England in 1625 would have had an easy task, but neither civil war in the country nor the death of the King was inevitable. The contests might have been settled by argument rather than by arms; even if the tension led to war, there was no need for the war to end in the sacrifice of the King. It was Charles's at once remarkable and tragic character, an exceptional firmness of purpose allied with an exceptional infirmity of judgment, which led to the final tragedy.

At the time of his accession he was in his twenty-fifth year, a small, well-made, sturdy young man whose considerable self-possession masked a natural shyness, betrayed only by a slight stammer. As a child he had been sickly, slow in walking and speaking, but his health had stabilized as he grew up, and although he was very small—an inch or so above five feet—he was strong, agile, a graceful dancer and a fine horseman.

The second son of King James by his Danish Queen, he was born at Dunfermline in November 1600 while his father was still King of Scots. After his father's accession to the English throne in 1603 he had come south and had been brought up there. He retained, however, his Scottish way of speech, though his accent was never so broad as his father's. He also showed in general a preference for Scots among his attendants. This was not altogether fortunate because his English breeding made him a stranger in Scotland while his Scottish preferences stood between him and his English subjects.

His elder brother Henry, the gallant and popular Prince of Wales, died suddenly in 1612, and Charles, who stepped into his place as heir-apparent, never at any time in his life acquired his brother's popularity. He had not the easy open

charm that pleased the multitude and he deliberately culti-
vated distance and dignity. It was typical of him that he had
suppressed the usual procession at his Coronation, not wanting to convert a sacred ceremony into a popular street show.

At the time of his accession he was enjoying one of his
few brief spells of comparative popularity. His father, with
the laudable but somewhat unrealistic intention of pacifying
Europe, had wished to marry him to the Infanta of Spain,
thus as he hoped uniting two nations which had long been
hostile. This policy was bitterly unpopular with the majority
of Protestant Englishmen who saw Spain as the protagonist
of the Counter-reformation in Europe and as the principal
opponent of English expansion overseas. Religious fervour
and economic interest alike prompted them in their hostility
to Spain. When therefore the young Prince, after visiting
Madrid, himself called off the alliance, returned home in
anger and forced his unwilling father to break with Spain, he
achieved a brief and gratifying popularity. Many believed
that he would, on his succession a year later, restore the lost
and legendary glories of Queen Elizabeth's reign.

The King deceived their expectations. He entrusted the
conduct of his wars to his father's favourite, now his own, the
Duke of Buckingham. Parliament, hating the Duke and
believing him incompetent, voted insufficient supplies for
the prosecution of the war. A series of disasters ensued, for
which the popular voice blamed the King and his too much
beloved minister. The murder of Buckingham in 1628 came
too late to restore confidence in Charles. Furthermore the
unconcealed joy of the populace at the death of his friend
deeply wounded the silent and sensitive young King, and
confirmed him in distrust and resentment of the common
people and their opinions.

After Buckingham's death the King assumed the guidance

of his own affairs. Unable to agree with his Parliaments, he dissolved the third of them in March 1629 and embarked on his experiment in personal government. His intentions were wholly benevolent; he wished to see his people firmly and justly governed and to keep them in sober order within the fold of one Church. But there were insurmountable difficulties in his path. He had, by dissolving Parliament, cut off his principal supply of money. In order to defray the expenses of government he resorted to practices which were dubiously legal and extremely unpopular. He revived certain mediaeval dues and compelled the gentry either to pay for the honour of knighthood or to pay fines for exemption from it. He instituted an inquiry into the enclosure of the ancient royal forests—a process which had been going on unquestioned for years—and imposed heavy fines on those who were guilty of encroachments. He granted to his courtiers monopolies of the manufacture or sale of various important commodities, tobacco, salt and soap among others. The monopolists freely employed searchers and informers to pry out any who tried to circumvent their rights, so that the King's government from end to end of the kingdom was associated with a system of spying and interference.

Finally he imposed ship-money, a special and time-honoured levy for the benefit of the navy. As long as this was collected only from sea-board counties he was within his established rights because the levy was justified by previous practice. But when he extended it to the inland counties, the new imposition could be challenged as illegal because he had not sought the authorization of Parliament to do so. Several of his opponents had been waiting for just this opportunity. Unable to make their voices heard in Parliament, since he would not call Parliament, they hoped to make their voices heard in the law courts. They refused to pay the tax and by so doing challenged the King to prosecute them. King Charles fell into the trap. He selected for his test case John Hampden a popular and influential Buckinghamshire landowner who had in earlier years been one of his opponents in Parliament. The judges who heard the case were not unanimous and although a majority were for the King, the open division of opinion was extremely damaging to the royal position.

There was, however, more to this question of ship-money than a mere matter of taxation. The King had undoubtedly hoped to build up his popularity by enlarging the Navy. Ships were surely something that the sea-faring English would be willing to pay for, and much propaganda had been made by his government for the launching of the largest warship yet built in England the majestic Sovereign of the Seas. Yet the people did not respond and the reason was not far to seek.

Unable to sustain wars abroad the King had begun his personal rule by making peace with Spain, and he had done so on terms which appalled his subjects. Spanish armies, in association with Austrian and Bavarian forces, were in the heart of Germany over-running and driving back the Protestant powers. The Protestant Dutch were still locked in the struggle with Spain which had lasted intermittently since 1567. Yet the King of England, to the disgust of his Protestant subjects, entered into an agreement with Spain to transport Spanish bullion for the payment of troops, and later even the troops themselves, in English vessels to the Netherlands. English ships were neutral and therefore immune from attack. In return for this service, a percentage of each cargo of bullion was paid into the English mint. The King therefore appeared to his subjects to be most unfairly and shamelessly favouring the might of Popish Spain against the hard-pressed Protestant cause in Europe. The belief was further stimulated by the King's friendly attitude to the Roman Catholic circle at his Court which clustered about his French wife, Queen Henrietta Maria.

His plans for increasing the Navy were therefore viewed with misgiving, since the use to which he would put his ships was by no means clear to his people. In effect, in 1640, the King actually put forward to the Spaniards a scheme by which the English Navy should regularly convey their troops and supplies to the Netherlands in return for the gigantic subsidy of four million ducats.

The King had thus provoked the mistrust of his subjects in civil affairs by vexatious interference and demands, and in foreign affairs by linking his policy to that of Spain. His church policy was even more unlucky. Sustained by William Laud, his able and energetic Archbishop, he sought to impose a decent uniformity of ceremonial. But many of his subjects thought all ceremonial Popish, while the Church had lost much of its authority with them through the poverty into which it had fallen since the plunder of the Reformation. Incessant and unseemly arguments over tithes brought the local clergy into disrepute; owing to the poverty of benefices, pluralism was rampant. Though some fine scholars and saintly men distinguished the Church at this epoch, its resources in men and money were wholly inadequate to the needs of the nation. Puritan lecturers occupied parish pulpits left vacant by absentee pluralists, while all over the country, prayer meetings in private houses and secret conventicles supplied the desperate spiritual thirst which the Church, through sheer lack of resources, was unable to satisfy. Puritan preachers were prosecuted in the Court of High Commission and, when they trenched on politics, in the Court of Star Chamber—the two prerogative Courts by which the King sought to enforce his policy. But this only exacerbated the problem by making martyrs of the Puritans. Nothing effective was done to attack the problem from the root.

The final and most serious problem was that of administration. The King had embarked on his experiment in personal government without the proper instruments to carry it out. He had no civil service to execute his commands. He depended on the local magnates great and small—Lord Lieutenants and sheriffs of counties, Justices of the Peace, parish constables. No order promulgated by the King in Council would take effect unless these people were willing and ready to carry it out. It was essential therefore that these people should be either in wholesome awe of the King and his Council, or in general agreement with his policy. In Queen Elizabeth's time they had been always in awe of her and usually in agreement with her. She took care that it should be so. Under King Charles, they were neither. He had, in the earlier part of his personal rule, attempted to establish a respect for his vigilant Council by insisting on regular six monthly reports from Justices of the Peace. But as neither Charles nor his Council appear to have taken any action on these, they soon lost all significance. He found his most energetic minister, Lord Wentworth, rather an embarrassment than otherwise, with his constant suggestions about administration and finance; in 1633 he sent him off to Ireland where he could find an outlet for his energies without troubling the King and his easy-going advisers at home.

In outward appearance the King's Court was impressive for its orderliness and ceremony. His collection of pictures and works of art was the finest in Europe and one of the finest that has ever existed. But he had no feeling for the art of government and no taste for the kind of work that government involves. On every major issue his judgment was at fault, and the first serious crisis which shook his precariously placed power was bound to bring it down.

A rebellion in Scotland against the Anglican ritual ended the King's dream in a rude awakening. His English subjects, in sympathy with the Scottish rebels, could not be brought to fight against them. The Scots invaded England, and to find the money to send them home, Charles was forced to call Parliament in November 1640.

The Long Parliament, as it came to be called, was led by John Pym one of the ablest Parliamentary organizers this country has ever known. His intention was clear. He wanted to compel the King to pass legislation which would render him dependent on Parliament and prevent any repetition of his experiment in personal government.

His first move was to destroy the King's only efficient advisers. Archbishop Laud was sent to the Tower; Wentworth, through the culpable weakness of the King, went to the block. This was the only time in his life when the King was over-persuaded to act against his conscience, and he regretted it openly and eloquently many times in the ensuing years. Pym's next move was to have the Prerogative Courts abolished, since these were the punitive weapon by which the King had enforced his policy during his absolute rule. When they were gone he would have no means of punishing dissidents except in the ordinary Courts and by the Common Law of the realm. The Common Law was by no means a bulwark of royal power.

For these reforms Pym had the majority of Parliament behind him and the King bowed to necessity. But Charles yielded only because he was forced to do so, and had no intention of permitting these infringements of his power to become permanent. Between the first and second session of the Long Parliament, in the summer of 1641, profiting by the natural revulsion of feeling in his favour, he planned a counter-attack on his opponents. He was bound to do so by his duty to his office.

John Pym, for his part, planned in the second session of Parliament to strike both the spiritual and temporal swords out of the royal hands, and so perpetuate the triumph of Parliament. He wanted the legal power of the Bishops excluded from Parliament; he wanted Parliament to have the power of approving the King's councillors and the control of the armed forces. A rebellion in Ireland and the necessity to raise an army to suppress it suddenly, in October 1641, made this question of the right to control the armed forces of immediate urgency. To counteract the mounting reaction in favour of the King, Pym in November 1641 worked up the Grand Remonstrance, a lengthy bulletin retailing the errors of the King's policy throughout his reign which was intended almost barefacedly as propaganda to show that he was unfit to be trusted. It passed the House of Commons by only eleven votes and was subsequently published in order to inflame the people. In the high state of public excitement, pamphlet warfare was already raging, and the first English newspapers began to appear in the autumn of 1641 and rapidly multiplied.

The close voting over the Grand Remonstrance had shown that Pym's majority in the House of Commons was no longer secure, and the King, hoping to make good use of the reaction in his favour, decided that the moment had come to strike. In January 1642 he came to the House of Commons in person at the head of his personal guards and attempted to arrest John Pym and four of his more vociferous colleagues. The accused men, forewarned, had already left the House and the King had to withdraw without them.

OLIVER CROMWELL

This ill-timed show of force was fatal to the King for it swung popular opinion violently away from him once more and restored Pym's control over the House of Commons.

The King withdrew from London, where he no longer felt himself safe. He was followed by repeated demands from Parliament that he pass a Militia Bill conceding to them the control of the armed forces. He refused and in the course of the summer he and Parliament separately put their claims into action by raising forces. Soon clashes occurred between their supporters, and the Civil War had virtually begun several weeks before the King formally raised his standard at Nottingham in August 1642.

The King's intention, had he won the Civil War, was to establish his unquestioned authority over all future parliaments. As he would have retained in his hands control over the armed forces, and would certainly not have disbanded his army until he had secured his position, he might in this way have achieved his ideal of unquestioned authority, and reduced Parliament to the status of an advisory body only. He would then have been able to resume his interrupted experiment in personal government having in his hands sufficient force to compel both tribute and obedience. This would have been one way out of the deadlock which had so long existed between King and Parliament: a solution in favour of a virtually absolute monarchy.

In the event of a Parliamentary victory the Parliamentary leaders imagined that they could compel the King to yield to their demands, and establish in England a limited monarchy under the control of Parliament. This would have been another way out of the deadlock. Unhappily they were entirely mistaken in their beliefs. The King had no intention of yielding to their demands in any circumstances whatsoever. Thus, in the event of a Parliamentary victory, no solution was possible while the King lived. From this, the final tragedy sprang.

By the spring of 1646 the King was utterly defeated in war. He took evasive action by escaping from his besieged headquarters at Oxford and surrendering not to the English Parliamentary army but to the Scots. The Scots had for the last two years been fighting as the allies of Parliament, but there were many differences between them, and the King had some reason for believing that he might break up the alliance and even resume the war against Parliament with Scottish help. This was by no means a foolish idea, and indeed it was strongly backed by the Queen, now in exile in France, by the French ambassador and even by the astute ruler of France, Cardinal Mazarin. The hopeful plan broke down because both the King and the Scots put conscience before personal advantage. The Scots would not support the King unless he agreed to accept the Presbyterian religion—which they fanatically believed to be the only true one—and impose it on his subjects. This the King utterly refused to do because the doctrines of the Presbyterian religion could not in any way be reconciled with his conception of Kingship. 'The nature of Presbyterian government is to steal or force the Crown from the King's head,' he wrote to his wife. It became evident within a few months that if he did not yield to them, they would hand him over, a helpless prisoner, to the victorious English Parliament.

In his now serious peril the King's extraordinary constancy began at last to shine clearly. In his previous troubles he had often seemed puzzled and hesitant, sure of his ultimate goal but fickle and easily swayed in his immediate policy. Now he had no doubts as to what he must do. His wife and her friends implored him to yield to the Scots: it was his only chance. The Scots themselves relentlessly harried, exhorted and preached at him. But his chief fear was that anxiety for his welfare might lead his friends to overrule him and make in his name, or possibly in that of his son, concessions that he could not approve. He wrote nobly from his imprisonment to the councillors of the Queen and the Prince of Wales: 'I conjure you by your unspotted faithfulness, by all that you love, by all that is good, that no threatenings, no apprehensions of danger to my person, make you stir one jot from any foundation in relation to that authority my Son is born to. I have already cast up what I am like to suffer, which I shall meet, by the Grace of God, with that constancy that befits me. Only I desire that consolation, that assurance from you, as I may justly hope that my cause shall not end with my misfortune, by assuring me that misplaced pity to me do not prejudice my Son's right.'

Morally defeated, the Scots handed the King over to his English enemies. It was 30th January 1647, two years to the day before his execution. Just before he went into this new captivity the King had sent a message to the Queen-regent of France, imploring her to recognize his cause as 'the cause of every King in Christendom' and to make his danger known to his fellow monarchs. He saw himself now as the solitary defender of the sacred rights of monarchy and was prepared to die for them.

But he had still an interlude of hope, for Parliament in England faced unmanageable problems. The war had been won for them by an Army imbued with religious fanaticism, an Army of which the moving spirit was Oliver Cromwell, 'the darling of the sectaries'. John Pym and John Hampden, the original leaders of the Parliamentary opposition, were long since dead. Parliament was divided between a moderate group leaning in religion towards a secular brand of Presbyterianism and the group known as the Independents, whose principal leader was Cromwell. The Independents were opposed to organized religion and belonged to a variety of different sects; they believed in toleration of a kind, and were closely linked to the Army in which many of them were officers. The so-called Presbyterians in the spring of 1647 dominated Parliament, while the Army was the striking force of Independency. In this division the King saw new cause for hope.

At first he was the prisoner of Parliament who held him in honourable confinement at Holmby House in Northamptonshire. It was here that Thomas Herbert began his faithful attendance on him. In June 1647 the King was suddenly seized by Cornet Joyce, an Independent officer, and taken to join the Army then near Newmarket. The Army's next move was to march on London; the leading Presbyterians fled from Parliament leaving the fate of the nation to the Army and its commanders. Thomas Fairfax was the commander-in-chief but no one doubted that his Lieutenant-General, Oliver Cromwell, was the real power behind these new developments. The Army encamped at Putney and the King was moved to Hampton Court. Here he was visited by his younger children, received many of his old friends, and entered into negotiations with the Army leaders.

The confused disaster of these negotiations is not easy to disentangle with justice to both parties. The King was certainly never in earnest on matters of principle because he could not agree to the limitations on his power which were contemplated. But he may have been in earnest in believing that he could win over Cromwell with promises of favour; he certainly went out of his way to charm the Puritan ladies, Mrs Cromwell and her daughter. It had always been a source of weakness to him that he misjudged men, and repeatedly imagined that they could be made to abandon their principles by offers of royal favour. He seems once again, and fatally, to have made this mistake with Cromwell. Whatever his other hopes of these negotiations, he used them also to gain time, and lost no opportunity of encouraging in secret other intrigues for his restoration—with the Scots, and with the English royalists.

It has been argued by Cromwell's enemies that he was not in earnest either but entangled the King with the deliberate intention of forcing him into a false position. This idea lies behind Marvell's lines:

> And Hampton shows what part
> He had of wiser Art,
> Where, twining subtile fears with hope,
> He wove a Net of such a scope,
> That Charles himself might chase
> To Caresbrooks narrow case.

It seems much more probable that Cromwell acted in good faith but misjudged both the sincerity of the King and his own power over the Army. The extremists in the Army had by now added to their demands for religious toleration, far-reaching demands for social justice. Their pleas, which included one for manhood suffrage, would have shaken not only the monarchy but the entire social order. Charles appears to have been genuinely perturbed by rumours that these extremists sought his life and might take the law into their own hands. At any rate he fled from Hampton Court on the night of 11th November 1647.

This action was fatal to him. It precipitated a mutiny in the Army which Cromwell brought under with difficulty. To hold the Army at all he must henceforward repudiate all his dealings with the King. Charles meanwhile had reached the Isle of Wight only to discover that the governor of Carisbrooke Castle, Colonel Hammond, could not be won from his fidelity to Parliament. The King was still a prisoner.

From this point onwards, our text takes up the story in Thomas Herbert's words. Herbert was not by any means aware of all the political circumstances which governed the King's fate, but he gives a vivid picture of his day to day life. Charles had in fact entered into a secret understanding with the Scots, conceding in this last desperate throw the temporary recognition of the Presbyterian religion. He reckoned, unwisely as it turned out, on a revulsion of feeling in his favour in England. He believed that the more moderate and conservative among his opponents were now thoroughly frightened by the extremists, and that a general rising in his favour was likely to succeed.

In May 1648, while he was ever more closely confined at Carisbrooke, the second Civil War broke out, stimulated by his secret encouragement. There were Royalist risings in South Wales, in Kent, Essex and the North, followed by an invasion from Scotland. Contrary to the King's hopes this second outburst of war, so far from rallying his subjects to his cause, hardened the hearts of many and virtually decided his fate.

Against the speedy and efficient Army, the Scots and the Royalists never had any real hope of success. But while Fairfax and Cromwell were fully occupied in the field, the Presbyterian members of Parliament, resumed control at Westminster. They re-opened negotiations with the King, and so took place the abortive discussions known as the Treaty of Newport, the manner and character of which Thomas Herbert describes. The King now appeared willing to make extensive though temporary concessions about the control of the armed forces and the state of the Church. But all the arguments at Newport proved meaningless, for as soon as the war was over, the Army repudiated the action taken by Parliament. On 16th November 1648, at a council of officers, the Army resolved to bring the King to justice for making war on his people. On 6th and 7th December, Colonel Pride and his troops guarded the approaches to Westminster and excluded from Parliament all who had supported the treaty with the King. The House of Commons was now reduced to a rump of about seventy members. The Treaty of Newport was swept aside and all was put in train for the trial of the King.

Every effort was made to make this trial appear legal, and every effort was in vain. The House of Commons had no legal right to set up a Court to try anyone, as Charles was quick to point out. In any case the remnant at Westminster was no free Parliament but a splinter group controlled by military force. It was difficult to find a president for the Court; all the leading lawyers of the Parliamentary party refused to act. It was necessary to fall back on a lawyer of modest distinction, a recently created serjeant-at-law and a Judge in Wales, John Bradshaw. For a minor man lifted suddenly to a position as prominent as it was difficult, Bradshaw surpassed expectation. He was calm, authoritative and dignified throughout, but legally speaking, the King invariably had the best of the argument.

Brought by force of arms before an illegal Court, Charles stood out with serene resolution as the defender of liberty and legality against the outrageous encroachments of the victorious Army. His own infringements or exploitations of the law during his absolute rule were trivial compared to the monstrously illegal course on which the Army and the Rump had now embarked. Charles recognized his last and greatest opportunity, and took it. By refusing to recognize the authority of the Court, he made it nearly impossible to proceed with the trial at all, and quite impossible to make it appear as anything but a travesty of justice.

The reader who brings an unprejudiced mind to this extraordinary event may, however, see much to admire in both parties. The King commands respect in his terrible predicament. Grey-haired, looking far older than his forty-eight years, worn with anxiety and hope deferred, he stood forth fearlessly, day after day, as the defender of his subjects' liberties and the laws of the land against arbitrary power. He had one argument only, but it was enough. He would not plead before a Court that had no authority under any known law. The last moment, after the passing of the sentence, is the most telling. He had evidently believed that he might speak, and found himself prevented: for a moment he became confused and showed a startled disappointment, then splendidly recovering himself he uttered his last devastating condemnation of his judges: 'I am not suffered for to speak. Expect what justice other people may have.'

On the other hand there is also something admirable in the tenacity of Bradshaw, in his utter refusal to be shaken in his assertion of the Court's authority. The law was not on his side, but by resolutely behaving as though it were, he was doing what he could to establish the principle that all men, even Kings, are answerable to law.

The full meaning of this trial and death of a King will never be rightly understood by those who take up vehemently with one party or the other. The King and the best of his opponents alike believed that they were doing right in the sight of God; they had come to this final confrontation because they refused to compromise with their convictions.

Many obscure causes and many accidents worked together

to bring about the tragedy. Economic changes had so modified the framework of society that its ancient institutions must either change or perish. Religious belief and political necessity had between them brought forth new theories of government to cover the new needs and experiences of society. Monarchy, as Charles conceived of it, was not, as he thought, the embodiment of an eternal truth but a new idea born from the struggles of the last hundred years. So too 'the ancient and fundamental laws and liberties of this nation' which his judges declared that he had infringed, were not ancient or fundamental at all, but were a series of misinterpretations of the law arrived at by applying mediaeval formulae to modern conditions.

It is rarely given to human beings to understand all the complexities of the situations in which they find themselves. The protagonists in this contest (as in so many others) acted blindly and often out of misapprehension. But the best of them on both sides acted honourably and bravely and in accordance with what they believed to be right. This honesty of purpose gives to the interchanges at the trial their extraordinary poignancy. It can be felt too in the upsurge of agonized doubt that inspired the intervention of poor John Downes who 'ought not to have been there at all'.

It was the tragedy of that epoch, as of many others, that the protagonists in the conflict would not recognize in the motives of their opponents the same moral fervour which characterized their own. So, to the Army leaders, Charles was a 'Man of Blood' who made war on his subjects out of a 'wicked design' to subvert the laws of the realm. So, to Charles, all his opponents were ambitious or venal or both. Hence his futile attempts to win Cromwell by favour; hence his words to the soldiers who insulted him as he left Westminster Hall: 'Poor soldiers, for a piece of money they would do so for their commanders'. The Christian compassion of the phrase is impressive, but it is a strangely blind comment on the character of that fanatic Army.

The trial and death of King Charles is one of the great political dramas of European history; to read of it in the words of contemporaries and eye-witnesses is to share in its intensity.

C. V. WEDGWOOD

FOREWORD

THE account of the trial and captivity of Charles I contained in this book is taken from two main sources: the memoirs of Sir Thomas Herbert and the Historical Collections of John Rushworth.

Sir Thomas Herbert (1606–82) was Groom of the Bedchamber to the King. He had travelled widely in India and the Middle East, and when the Civil War broke out he was inclined to the side of Parliament. He was appointed by that body to attend the King during his captivity and served him, with great devotion, until his execution. He was rewarded for this by the grant of a baronetcy at the Restoration, and in 1678 he published the first draft of these memoirs under the title of *Threnodia Carolina*.

John Rushworth (1612?–90) was a lawyer who deliberately collected information about state affairs because they interested him. In 1642 he was appointed clerk-assistant to the House of Commons, and later served as secretary to Fairfax and, for a short time, Cromwell. He was very well placed for accumulating documents and recording authentic impressions of the events of these troubled years, and his *Historical Collections*, which were published at intervals from 1659, are one of the most important primary sources for the history of this period.

Three long extracts from Herbert and two from Rushworth have been linked to form a continuous narrative, combining the personal recollections of the one, with the detached, more official, account of the other; spelling and punctuation have been occasionally altered, in order to avoid confusion, and brief footnotes are provided to elucidate difficulties in the text and to give a minimum of information about the more important people who are mentioned. Longer notes, quoting from other sources, are included as appendices.

R.L.

PART I

FROM CARISBROOK CASTLE
TO ST JAMES'S

Sir Thomas Herbert's Account

O N the 13th of November 1647 the King crossed the sea, was safe landed at Cowes in the Isle of Wight, where Colonel Hammond,* the Governor was attending, and passed through Newport (the principal town in that Island). The Governor, with alacrity and confidence, conducted his Majesty to Carisbrook Castle, attended only by Sir John Berkeley,† and two gentlemen, his servants. Sure I am, many that cordially loved the King, did very much dislike his going to this place, it being so remote, and designed neither for his Honour nor safety; as the consequence proved. A gentle-woman, as his Majesty passed through Newport, presented him with a damask rose which grew in her garden at that cold season of the year, and prayed for him, which his Majesty heartily thanked her for.

Carisbrook Castle is the only place of defence within that

*Robert Hammond (1621–54) married John Hampden's daughter, fought for Parliament in the Civil War and had at first supported Cromwell. As Cromwell's attitude towards the King hardened, Hammond's confidence in him declined and he was glad to retire from active military life to the Governorship of the Isle of Wight.

†Sir John Berkeley (1606–78) served with distinction in command of the Royalist forces in the West Country. He attempted to mediate between the King and the Army but was not trusted by the Army leaders. He went into exile in France until the Restoration. His brother, Sir William Berkeley, was Governor of Virginia.

Island, albeit upon the Marine the Isle hath many forts or block houses. Its name is derived from Whitgare, a Saxon, corruptly contracted to Garisbrook. The Isle being subdued at the Conquest by William Fitz Osborne, Earl of Hereford, he built this Castle, which in King Henry III's time was enlarged by Isabel de Fortibus, sister and heir to Baldwin, Earl of Devon and Albemarle, who founded there a Priory, dedicated to St Mary Magdalen, for Benedictines or Black Monks, as we call them. The Castle was new built (or enlarged rather) by Order of King Henry VIII and by Queen Elizabeth regularly fortified; so as the out works are large, and planted with great ordnance, and has served as a place of retreat for the Islanders against the French and Spaniard, when the English were in war with them.

Thither (so soon as the King's being there was rumoured) repaired several of his old servants, and some new, such as his Majesty at that time thought fit to nominate (for some weeks there was no prohibition, any that were desirous to see his Majesty might without opposal) or that, according to the duty of their place, were to give their attendance. His Majesty had free liberty to ride and recreate himself any where within the Isle, when and where he pleased; the only want was, that his Chaplains, Dr Sheldon and Dr Hammond, were not long tolerated to perform their Office, which was no little grief to him, in regard he had no disposition to hear those that exercised according to the Directory* which was then practised. But they hindered not his private Devotion, which every day he carefully attended, and the Lord's Day he observed, by reading the Bible, and other books fitting him for Prayer and Meditation in his Oratory.

*A book of directions for public worship in the Presbyterian manner drawn up by an assembly of divines at Westminster in 1644 after the suppression of the Book of Common Prayer.

Howbeit, this liberty of refreshing in the Isle abroad was of no long duration; for about the middle of February, Colonel Hammond, the Governor (soon after the King arose from dinner) came into the Presence, which was under his Majesty's Bedchamber, and in solemn manner addressed himself to the King. After a short preamble he said he was sorry to acquaint his Majesty with the orders he received the night before from his superiors, and then pausing a while, the King bid him speak out. The Governor replied his orders were to forbid Mr Ashburnham, Mr Leg and the rest of his servants that were with him at Oxford, any further waiting on his person in that Castle and Garrison, the jealousies and apprehensions of those times judging it inconvenient to continue such in their attendance about his person.

The King, by his short silence, seemed surprised and, by his countenance, appeared to be troubled. Such as were at that time in the Presence noted it; but not knowing the occasion of his Majesty's sadness, they seemed full of grief, as by their dejected looks was visible. But the King beckoning with his hand to Mr Ashburnham and some others, he told them what the Governor had communicated, and what he expected not, nor was agreeable to what some considerable persons had promised. But no remedy but patience, which in these straits he commonly had recourse unto, and is the noble way of overcoming.

His Majesty's servants were much perplexed, and knew it would be to no purpose to expostulate with Colonel Hammond. The only comfort remaining was, that they were not excluded their royal master's affection, which supported them. Next day after the King had dined, those gentlemen came all together, and prostrating themselves at his Majesty's feet, prayed God for his preservation, and kissing his hand, departed.

This done, the day following a restraint began of the

King's going any more abroad into the Isle of Wight, his Majesty being then confined to Carisbrook Castle and Line without, albeit within the Works,* a place sufficiently large and convenient for the King's walking and having good air, and a delightful prospect both to the sea and land. For his Majesty's solace and recreation, the Governor converted the Barbacan, (a spacious parading ground within the Line, though without the Castle) into a Bowling Green, scarce to be equalled, and at one side built a pretty summer house, for retirement. At vacant hours these afforded the King most recreation, for the building within the Castle Walls had no Gallery, nor rooms of state, nor Garden, so as his Majesty, constantly in the forenoons, exercised himself in the Walks without, and in the afternoons there also, and in the Bowling green or Barbacan. Nevertheless both times he carefully observed his usual times set apart for his Devotion and for writing. Mr Harrington and Mr Herbert continued waiting on his Majesty in the Bedchamber: he gave Mr Herbert the charge of his books, of which the King had a catalogue, and from time to time had brought unto him, such as he was pleased to call for. The sacred Scripture was the Book he most delighted in, read often in Bishop Andrew's *Sermons*, Hooker's *Ecclesiastical Polity*, Dr Hammond's *Works*, Villalpandus upon Ezekiel, etc. Sands's *Paraphrase upon King David's Psalms*, Herbert's *Divine Poems*; and also *Godfry of Bulloigne*, writ in Italian by Torquato Tasso and done into English Heroic Verse by Mr Fairfax, a Poem his Majesty much commended, as he did also *Ariosto* [translated] by Sir John Harington,† a facetious Poet, much esteemed of by Prince

*i.e. Within the outer line of defence, built by Gianibelli in 1597, which was itself surrounded by the earthworks.
†Sir John Harington (1561–1612), godson of Elizabeth, was for some time tutor to Prince Henry.

Henry his Master;* Spencer's *Faerie Queen* and the like, for alleviating his spirits after serious studies. And at this time it was (as is presumed) he composed his Book called *Suspiria Regalia*, published soon after his Death, and entitled *The Kings Portraiture, in his Solitudes and Sufferings*, which manuscript Mr Herbert found amongst those books his Majesty was pleased to give him (those excepted which he bequeathed to his children hereafter mentioned). In this regard Mr Herbert did not see the King write that book, his Majesty being always private when he writ, and those his servants never coming into the Bedchamber when the King was private until he called; yet comparing it with his hand writing in other things, found it so very like, as induces his belief that it was his own hand writing. To instance a particular, there was his Majesty's translation of Dr Saunderson, the late Bishop of Lincoln's book *de Juramentis*, or like title concerning Oaths, all of it translated into English, and writ with his own hand. This in his Bedchamber, he was pleased to show his servants, Mr Harrington† and Mr Herbert, and commanding them to examine it with the Original, they found it accurately translated. His Majesty not long after shewed it the Bishop of London, Dr Juxon and also Dr Hammond and Dr Sheldon, his Majesty's Chaplains in Ordinary (which first and last were afterwards Archbishops of Canterbury) such time as they waited upon him at Newport in the Isle of Wight, during the Treaty.‡ In many of his books, he delighted himself with the

*Prince Henry, the eldest son of James I, born in 1594, died of fever in 1612, leaving his brother Charles heir to the throne.
†James Harrington (1611–77), political theorist and author of *Oceana*, took no active part in the Civil War but was appointed to accompany the King in captivity. He was a convinced republican but became, nevertheless, a close personal friend of the King.
‡The Treaty of Newport, the name given to the negotiations between King and Parliament in September 1648.

motto *Dum Spiro Spero*;* which he wrote frequently as the emblem of his hopes as well as endeavours for a happy agreement with his Parliament. A harmony and good accommodation he heartily desired, and a fair end to all matters that made this unhappy separation. Meantime he alleviated his mind by an honourable and cheerful submission to the Almighty, who in His wisdom orders and disposes all things according to His good pleasure, and who, in all his trials during his disconsolate condition, marvellously supported him with an unparallelled patience. In one of his books he writ this distich;

> *Rebus in adversis facile est contemnere vitam:*
> *Fortiter ille facit qui miser esse potest.*†

And out of another poet, against the levelling and anti-monarchic spirits which predominated at that time;

> *Fallitur egregio quis quis sub Principe credit*
> *Servitium; numquam Libertas gratior extat,*
> *Quam sub Rege pio,* ——— Claudian.‡

With many others which are memorable, and express his delight in Learning. For he understood authors in the originals, whether Greek, Latin, French, Spanish, or Italian, which three last he spoke perfectly; and none better read in Histories of all sorts, which rendered him accomplished, and also would discourse well in Arts and Sciences, and indeed not unfitted for any subject.

Notwithstanding this restraint, which the Governor was

---

*While I live, I hope.
†In adversity it is easy to pour scorn on life: he acts bravely, who can bear to be wretched.
‡He is mistaken who thinks that submission to a good prince is slavery; never does liberty show more charm than beneath a pious king.

strict in (probably in pursuance of his instructions) neverthe-less several diseased persons, troubled with the Evil resorted thither from remote parts to be touched;* and after some stay in Newport or other villages about, made means to get within the Line, and when the King went out of the Castle, towards his usual Walk about the Barbacan, they had their wished opportunity to present themselves afore him, and he touched them.

About this time one Mr Sedgwick (sometime Preacher in the Parliament Army) came to Carisbrook Castle, and de-sired Colonel Hammond the Governor's leave to address himself to the King. Mr Harrington being acquainted with the occasion, told his Majesty that a Minister was purposely come from London, to discourse with him about his spiritual concerns, and was desirous to present his Majesty with a book he had lately writ for his Majesty's perusal, which (as the gentleman said) if his Majesty would please to read, he sup-posed might be of much advantage to him, and comfort in that his uncomfortable condition. The King thereupon came forth, and Mr Sedgwick, in decent manner gave his Majesty the book, the title whereof was *Leaves of the Tree of Life*, being an explication of the second verse of the 22nd Chapter of the Revelation of St John. His Majesty, after he had read some part thereof, returned it with this short admonition and judg-ment: That by what he had read in that book, he believed the composer stood in some need of sleep. The King's advice being taken in the best sense, the Minister departed with seeming satisfaction.

Next day one Mr Harrington, a gentleman of a fair estate near Bath in Somerset shire (son to Sir John Harington,

---

*The King's Evil, the name given to scrofula which was popularly regarded as curable by royal touch. The practice of touching died out in England after the Stuarts.

afore-mentioned) came in like sort to Carisbrook Castle, upon the same charitable account. But his Majesty, having heard something concerning him, thanked him likewise for his good intentions, having no mind to enter into discourse with him upon controversial points; so as that gentleman also returned next homewards, having first wished the King much happiness.

His Majesty having thought fit to send a gracious message to his two Houses of Parliament, in the evening he gave it, sealed up, (and directed to the Speaker of the House of Lords *pro tempore*) to his servant Mr Herbert, with a letter to his daughter the Princess Elizabeth, who was then at St James's House near Whitehall with her Governess. The wind was not favourable, so as Mr Herbert had much ado to cross the sea from Cowes to Southampton; but in regard the King had ordered to make haste, so as the letter might be delivered next day before the House rose, no delay was suffered. Being landed he immediately took post for London. It may not be forgotten, that at one stage, the Post-Master (a malevolent person) having notice that the packet came from the King, and required extraordinary speed, mounted Mr Herbert upon a horse that had neither good eyes nor feet, so as he usually stumbled very much, which, with the deep ways (being winter) and dark night, in all probability might have abated his speed, but (through God's Goodness) the horse (though at his full gallop most part of that twelve miles riding) neither stumbled nor fell, which at the next stage was admired. The King's packet was delivered to the Lord Grey of Warke (at that time Speaker to the Lords House) within the time limited; which done, he waited upon the Princess Elizabeth, then at St James's, who gave him her hand to kiss, being overjoyed with her Royal Father's kind letter, to which she returned another by Mr Herbert, who had the King's approbation at his coming to Carisbrook, for his diligence.

I formerly hinted, that during the time that Dr Sheldon (afterwards Archbishop of Canterbury) and Dr Hammond, his Majesty's Chaplains in Ordinary, were permitted to wait at Carisbrook Castle, they performed the Service afore the King; howbeit their stay was but short, the Governor giving them unexpectedly a dismiss. The King thenceforth was Chaplain to himself not thinking fit to accept any Minister of the Presbytery, albeit he returned them thanks, and was civil to them.

Amongst others of that judgment (conforming to the Directory)* was one Mr Troughton, a young man and, I think, a graduate in one of our Universities, who (during his Majesty's confinement in Carisbrook Castle) was Chaplain to the Governor, and Preacher to the officers and soldiers in that Garrison. He seldom failed to be in the Presence Chamber when the King dined, delighting to see the King and, though he was but young, yet was he a student, and could argue pretty well in defence of some tenets he held in opposition to some ceremonies he had seen practised in Churches and discipline in the Episcopacy. The King usually, after meals, would walk for near an hour, and take many turns in the Presence Chamber, and pleasureably enter into disputation with Mr Troughton, who was very earnest in maintaining his arguments. The King never discouraged him, but being the better logician, had the advantage, and being better read in history and controversial points, gained ground of his opponent. The King always parted merrily, and was very pleasant; but one time, during their discourse, this young disputant standing at one end of the room, between a Lieutenant of Foot (who had his sword in his hand and was earnestly hearkening to their debate) and a gentleman that was not

*See footnote p. 32.

known to many there, the King in the heat of his discourse, took the officer's sword out of his hand so unexpectedly, as made the officer look strangely, and then drawing it, affrighted the disputant, he not imagining the reason, until the gentleman (better understanding the meaning) fell presently upon his knee, and his Majesty laying the sword upon his shoulder, conferred upon him the Honour of Knighthood, telling him, It was to perform a promise to his relations. That young Gentleman* is since advanced to greater honour and office under our Sovereign.

From Carisbrook Castle his Majesty sent some Proposals to the Parliament, who returned Four Preliminary Articles† (which the Scots Commissioners disrelished and the King disliked, as improper to precede a Treaty) which occasioned a stricter guard, and that vote of making no further address, which nevertheless was soon after repealed. And about the middle of August 1648 the Earl of Middlesex was sent by the House of Lords, and Sir John Hippersley and Mr John Bulkeley from the House of Commons, to present the King

*Sir John Duncomb.
†Charles proposed, among other things, the acceptance of a Presbyterian system of church government for a trial period of three years. Parliament replied by laying down four conditions which the King must accept before they would allow him to come to London to treat personally with them. These were (i) that Parliament should have authority over the army for twenty years and, indirectly, for all time to come. (ii) That the King should revoke his declarations against Parliament and (iii) annul the honours he had recently granted. (iv) That Parliament should have the right to adjourn itself to any place it thought desirable.

Charles was, at the same time, negotiating with the Scots. He accepted the Scottish terms (the Engagement) and rejected the Four Preliminary Articles. Parliament replied by passing the vote of No Addresses, in February 1648, breaking off all negotiations with the King. This was repealed the following May.

with the Votes of both Houses of Parliament, for a personal Treaty with his Majesty upon the propositions tendered at Hampton Court,* and a Committee of Lords and Commons at such times as his Majesty should think fit to appoint, and to be with honour and safety to his Royal Person.

The King, in the first place, gave them his hand to kiss, and then told them that their address being in order to peace, doubled their welcome, peace being the thing he earnestly desired. He assured them withal, that if upon the Treaty peace did not ensue, it should be no fault of his; he would not be blamed.

In order thereto, his Majesty was pleased to write back unto his Parliament, signifying the receipt of their late Votes; declaring withall, that he would treat with such of their Members as they should think fit to nominate and appoint to meet at Newport in the Isle of Wight; engaging withall, his Royal Word, that he would not depart out of the Island during the Treaty (which was limited to six weeks time) nor in three weeks after.

Pursuant whereto, several Lords and Members of the House of Commons, namely, the Earls of Northumberland, Pembroke, Salisbury, and Middlesex, Viscount Say and Sele, the Lord Winman, Mr Pierpoint, Mr Hollis, Mr Crew, Sir Henry Vane junior, Sir Harbottle Grimstone, Sir John Pots, Serjeant† Glynne, Serjeant Browne, Mr Bulkeley, with some others, were appointed by the two Houses of Parliament to repair forthwith to Newport and treat with his Majesty upon certain propositions.

*These propositions, originally presented by Parliament to Charles in 1646, demanded the abolition of Episcopacy and the establishment of a Presbyterian system in England.
†The name given to a member of a superior order of barristers (abolished in 1880) from which the Common Law judges were always chosen.

His Majesty (as soon as he was advertised that the Commissioners were on their way) removed from Carisbrook (which was to him a place of cares) to a gentleman's house in Newport, which was accommodated to his business so well as that small place would afford, albeit disproportionate and of small receipt for a Court. The King's old servants having then liberty to attend, several Lords and Gentlemen of the Bedchamber, namely, the Duke of Richmond, the Marquis of Hartford, the Earls of Southampton and Lindsey, Lord High Chamberlain, with others of the Nobility, likewise repaired thither, as also the Grooms of the Bedchamber, Pages of the Backstairs, and other servants that had offices; all which were permitted their attendance. Several of the King's Chaplains came thither also; Dr Hammond, Dr Sheldon, Dr Juxon, Dr Holdsworth, Dr Sanderson, Dr Turner, as also Sir Thomas Gardiner, Sir Orlando Bridgman, Mr Holborn, Mr Palmer and Mr Vaughan, etc. and with the Commissioners came Mr Marshall, Mr John Caril, Mr Richard Vines, and Mr Seaman. Mr Nye was there also, and some others, who (as occasion required) preached afore the Commissioners; and albeit the King would not accept of them amongst his Chaplains either praying or preaching, his Majesty was nevertheless affable to them, and said they were welcome, always desiring (as he has published) those pious assistances, which holy and good Ministers either Prelates or Presbyters could afford him, especially in those extremities, which God had pleased to permit some of his subjects to reduce him to.

Great rejoicing there was on all hands for this Convention, and fair hopes appeared that God would vouchsafe to give His blessing to it.

The Court being thus settled, and the most convenient house Newport could afford prepared (the town indeed is large, and of many streets, but the building none of the best, yet gave sufficient accommodation to that great concourse of men, as also to some foot companies that were quartered there) the King, so soon as the Lords and Gentlemen that came from the two Houses of Parliament had kissed his Majesty's hand and reposed a little while after their land and sea travel, met them at the appointed place. All being set, the King under a State* at the end of the room, the Parliament Commissioners at some distance on either side the Board and several Lords, and the King's Chaplains (Dr Sheldon, Dr Holdsworth, Dr Hammond, Dr Sanderson, Dr Turner, and the Bishop of London, as also Dr Morley) standing behind the King's Chair, he forthwith entered to treat with them upon their proposals, and a fair progress was made therein by his Majesty's ready condescension, especially in what related to Civil Affairs, wherein the Commissioners, pursuant to their Instructions, were principally concerned. His Majesty had also some conferences with the Assembly Divines, Mr Marshall and the other three lately named, in which was controverted some different Judgments referring to the ingenuous and true sense the Primitive Fathers had of Bishop and Presbyter, how understood as to their Administrations; for as to the Office of Deacons, that was agreed by both, but in the other their opinions differed. However, in these debates there were no heats on either side, but managed with great sobriety and moderation. And in all this Treaty his Majesty was observed in the whole transaction, both with the Commissioners and Divines, to keep a constant decorum, with great prudence, cautiousness, and good order. And albeit he was single, and obliged to answer what the Commissioners (who were many) had in Proposition or Objection, his Majesty's answers were pertinent, and delivered without

*i.e. Statecloth: the canopy over a throne.

any perturbation or show of discomposure, albeit he had to do with Persons, as of high civility and observance to the King, so of great parts and understanding in the Law and Affairs of State, and both for their ingenuity and fair carriage much commended by the King, as occasion afterwards offered.

The Propositions sent from the two Houses of Parliament to treat upon with the King, were eleven in number.

The *First* was, that the King should forthwith call in all such Proclamations and Declarations as his Majesty had at any time, during the late War, issued against the Proceedings of the two Houses of Parliament; to which the King agreed, provided, that neither this concession, nor any other of his upon this Treaty, should be of any force, unless the whole were agreed.

The *Second* was concerning the settlement of the Church, as to his confirming the Assembly of Divines sitting in the Abbey of Westminster, and to a settling of the Directory, and establishing of the Presbyterian Government for three years. Reserving, nevertheless, to himself and his party a liberty to use the old form,* his Majesty agreed. But as to the abolishing Episcopacy, and that hierarchy, or to the alienating the Church lands, or any part thereof, his Majesty would by no means give his assent.

To the *Third* Proposal, his Majesty was willing to permit the Parliament to have the Militia in their hands for twenty years.

To the *Fourth*, for nulling the Cessation† in Ireland, and leaving for some time the Government both Civil and Mili-

*i.e. The Prayer Book.
†The agreement between Ormond, the Royalist commander in Ireland, and the rebellious Catholic Confederation, which left the greater part of Ireland in the hands of the Catholics.

tary in the hands of his two Houses of Parliament, the King agreed.

To the *Fifth* and *Sixth* Proposals, for vacating Titles of Honour conferred since his Majesty's Great Seal was carried from London to Oxford;* and for payment of public debts, the King gave his assent.

To the *Seventh*, that delinquents† (that is those of his Party) should submit unto a fine, and be prohibited access unto the Court, as also unto the Council without the Parliament's Consent; and likewise, that for three years they should be disabled and debarred from sitting in either House of Parliament without their consent; and also to undergo a legal trial, if the two Houses of Parliament thought fit, and to suffer according to merit, if convicted by due course of law. Thus far his Majesty was willing to agree; but as to the charging them, or any of them, with Treason, or as to the taking away their or any of their lives or estates for acting things by his Commission during the late War in a military way or any other (save such as after a legal proceeding should be found guilty of breaking the established Laws of the Land) the King positively refused to give his assent.

To the *Eighth* Proposal his Majesty agreed; that the Parliament should have power to confer all offices in his Kingdom, and likewise constitute Magistrates for twenty years.

To the *Ninth*, for his confirming their new Broad Seal, with all Grants and Commissions past under the same, the King agreed.

---

*Lord Keeper Littleton fled to Charles at York in 1642, taking the Great Seal with him. It was later removed to Oxford, the Royalist capital. Parliament ordered a new one (the Broad Seal) to be made.

†The name applied by Parliament to all those who assisted the King. Their estates were ordered to be confiscated and sold to meet the expenses of Parliament.

To the *Tenth* Proposal, that all Charters, Grants, Privileges, and Immunities, with power to dispose of the Tower of London be ratified, the Militia there confirmed, and the citizens of London exempted from military duty and service out of their liberties,* unless ordered by the two Houses of Parliament, the King agreed.

To the *Eleventh*, that the Court of Wards† should be abolished, his Majesty having yearly one hundred thousand pounds paid him in composition or compensation thereof, his Majesty agreed.

The Treaty having this fair aspect, it was the judgment as well as wishes, of all such as were lovers of peace, that King and Parliament would now unite; and the rather, for that the Lords, upon the Report made unto them by their Commissioners in this Negotiation, voted that what the King had condescended to seemed to them satisfactory; and in the Commons House, after a long, and sharp debate, it was carried by majority of voices,‡ that his Majesty's answers and concessions were a ground sufficient and satisfactory for the Parliament to proceed upon, in order to a settlement of the Kingdom's peace.

These resolves made most men likewise verily believe there would be a happy union and agreement between his Majesty and the Parliament; and that these long and sharp contests in Civil War (if it may properly be so called where families are sadly divided, and estates unnaturally destroyed) would now be wound up in a peaceful conclusion.

But as his Majesty well observed, jealousies are not so

---

*A geographical term referring to the district, extending beyond the grounds of the City, over which the Corporation of London had control.
†Established by Henry VIII to deal with questions arising from the Crown's feudal rights over royal wards. It was abolished in 1660.
‡129 to 83.

easily allayed as raised. For albeit, his heart (he said) inclined sincerely to whatsoever might advance piety and peace amongst his people, yet the crying sins of this nation (as the sequel manifested) had so heightened God's indignation, as those good hopes and expectations were suddenly blasted. Peace, upon that score, being by some unquiet spirits, then in power, judged unsafe and inconvenient, so as the object, be it never so beautiful, if it do but thwart their design, shall be looked upon as deformed. And his Majesty has this expression upon record: '*God knows, and time will certainly discover, who are most to blame for the unsuccessfulness of that Treaty, the product of many succeeding calamities.*'

His Majesty was vehemently persuaded by some to leave the Island for his more safety, the times having an ill aspect towards him; but no arguments could prevail with him to violate his parole, as formerly hinted.

Now, in regard there are sundry relations published of the matters that ensued, as also of the force that was soon after put upon the House of Commons,* by some Officers of the Army, and whence influenced, as also of their garrisoning Whitehall with two Foot Regiments, and upon what design, is needless to be repeated here, the scope of this relation being only to give the occurrents of such court passages as this relater was an eyewitness to, and in reference to his observation of the sad and direful effects following.

While matters hung thus in suspense, the King nevertheless seemed confident, that for as much as his concessions were

---

*i.e. Pride's Purge. The army feared that Parliament's negotiations with the King would put the Presbyterians in power and lead to the dismissal of soldiers without guarantees of pay or of Independency (a forebear of modern Congregationalism). Colonel Pride, therefore, on the orders of a group of army officers, surrounded the House of Commons with troops on December 6, 1648 and kept out the Presbyterian majority, only permitting entry to the Independent minority.

voted satisfactory to the majority of both Houses of Parliament, the conclusion would be answerable, as to a firm and
lasting Peace. But, alas! In opposition thereto, Lieutenant
Colonel Cobbet, an officer in Colonel Fortescue's Regiment
(Joyce* like) came unexpectedly to Newport with a commanded Party of Horse, and, in the first place made enquiry
for Colonel Hammond's Quarters in the town, having
order to secure him, the reason unknown, unless from an
apprehension the despotic agitators† had, that he was too
much a courtier, which they approved not of. Howbeit,
being premonished he evaded him, though very narrowly.
But in this conjecture they were mistaken, albeit by his constant walking and discoursing with the King, whensoever his
Majesty, for refreshment, walked about the Works at Carisbrook (there being none so fit nor forward as he, being
Governor), gave him the opportunity to ingratiate himself
into his Majesty's favour, and made the Army officers jealous
of him, being solely intrusted with the person of the King.
Nevertheless he forfeited the King's good opinion, by that
uncomely act of looking into his scrutore,‡ to search for some
supposed papers of Intelligence from the Queen, and corre-
spondency with others, wherein he missed his aim. Mr Harrington and Mr Herbert were then in the Green, waiting on
the King who, finding the weather somewhat cold, bid Mr
Herbert go for his cloak; and entering the Bedchamber, they
found the Governor ready to come forth, with one other

*Cornet Joyce had been sent by Cromwell in June, 1647 to carry off
Charles from Parliament's control at Holmby House and to conduct him
to Newmarket.
†i.e. The army officers, led by Fairfax and Cromwell. Hammond had, in
fact, already been recalled and was under temporary arrest at Windsor
when Cobbet arrived at Newport.
‡Writing cabinet, from the French *escritoire*. This incident had taken
place before the arrival of Cobbet.

officer in company, and Mr Reading, who then waited as Page of the Backstairs, and by insinuation had let him in. Mr Herbert, as he was returning to the Green with his Majesty's cloak, gave the Page a sharp rebuke, which the Governor being acquainted with, threatened Mr Herbert to give him a dismiss, for censuring that act of his; and without doubt, had expelled him the Castle, if his Majesty, of his goodness, had not passed it by, without either reproaching the Governor, or taking notice thereof. Those, with some other aggravations, made the King design an escape, horses being provided and laid near the Castle, and a vessel made ready for his transportation. But by a corrupted Corporal in the Garrison, it took not effect, and a Providence was therein, his person being hazarded if he made the attempt; and for it an officer had his trial afterwards by due course of Law, upon a charge of High Treason, as the history of those times mentions.*

But to Newport return; Lieutenant-Colonel Cobbet, failing of his first design of apprehending Colonel Hammond, he made a higher flight in the next place, making an abrupt address unto the King, letting him know that he had Orders to remove him forthwith from Newport. The King beheld the Lieutenant-Colonel with astonishment, and interrogated him whether his order was to remand him back to his Prison at Carisbrook? The Lieutenant said no. Whither then, said the

*This seems to refer to the second attempt, of May 1648, when Charles planned to cut through the iron bar of his window and escape from the castle with the connivance of three of the soldiers. But two of these informed the Governor and the plan was frustrated. One of the officers of the garrison, Major Rolph, was accused of urging Charles to escape, with the intention of shooting him. He was tried for this on a charge of high treason but was acquitted. He returned to Carisbrook and was one of the three deputy governors in control when Cobbet arrived to remove Charles in November 1648. It may well have been Rolph, sore at his treatment, and not Cobbet, who tried to force his way into the royal coach as Herbert relates below.

King? Out of the Isle of Wight replied the Colonel; but the place he was to remove the King unto, he was not to communicate. I pray Sir, by your favour (said the King) let me see your orders. As to that, the Lieutenant-Colonel desired to be excused. This business (said he), is of no ordinary concernment, so as I may not satisfy any man's enquiry until a fitter season. Now was verified his Majesty's maxim, that such as will assume the boldness to adventure upon a King, must not be thought over modest or timorous to carry on his design. His Majesty being thus denied a sight, demanded if his orders or instructions were from Parliament or the General of their Army?* His answer was, he had them from neither, nor from any else. 'It may be so,' (said the King) 'seeing you are afraid to show them.' But that he had orders, or secret instructions for this bold act, is not to be doubted; for though there was but one General, yet things were at that time so much out of frame, both in the Commons House and Army, as there were many commanders.

The Duke of Richmond, the Lord High Chamberlain, the Lord Marquis of Hartford, with others of the Nobility, several venerable persons, and many of the King's Household servants at that time attending, were in a manner confounded at this surprise and unexpected accident; yea, not a little affrighted with ideas and apprehensions of danger to his Majesty's person; and the more for that the Lieutenant-Colonel refused to satisfy any, to what place he would go, or what he intended to do with the King, other than that no harm or violence should be offered him.

The Lieutenant-Colonel pressed the King to take coach; the coach accordingly was made ready and brought to the door where the King lodged.

Never, at one time, 'tis thought, was beheld more grief in

*Fairfax.

men's faces, or greater fears in their hearts, the King being at such a time, and in such a manner hurried away they knew not whither; but no remedy appearing, the noblemen, the venerable persons, and other his Majesty's servants, approached to kiss the King's hand, and to pour forth their supplications to Almighty God to safeguard and comfort his Majesty in that his disconsolate condition.

His Majesty, who at other times was cheerful, at his parting from his friends showed sorrow in his heart, by the sadness of his countenance; a real sympathy.

The King now ready to take coach, asked the Lieutenant-Colonel, whether he was to have any servants with him? Only such (said he) as are most useful. The King then nominated Mr Harrington and Mr Herbert to attend in his Bedchamber, and scarce a dozen more for other service. The King taking notice that Mr Herbert had for three days absented himself, Mr Harrington told his Majesty, he was sick of an ague. He then desired the Duke of Richmond to send one of his servants to see in what condition he then was, and if any thing well, to come along with him. The gentlemen the Duke sent found him sweating; but so soon as he received the message, arose and came speedily to his Majesty, who soon took coach, and commanded Mr Harrington, Mr Herbert, and Mr Mildmay, his carver, to come into his coach, and the Lieutenant-Colonel offering to enter the coach uninvited, his Majesty (by opposing his foot) made him sensible of his rudeness, so as with some shame he mounted his horse, and followed with a Guard of Horse, the coachman driving as he directed.

The King in this passage showed no discomposure at all, but would be asking the Gentlemen in the coach with him, whither they thought he was travelling? They made some simple replies, such as served to make his Majesty smile at their innocent conjectures; otherwhile could comfort himself with what he had granted at his late Treaty with the Commissioners, whom he highly praised for their ingenuity and fair deportment at Newport, as formerly mentioned.

The coach (by the Lieutenant-Colonel's directions) went westwards towards Worsley Tower in Freshwater Isle a little beyond Yarmouth Haven; thereabout his Majesty rested, until the vessel was ready to take him aboard, a sorrowful spectacle, and great example of Fortunes inconstancy. The wind and tide favouring, they crossed that narrow sea in three hours, and landed at Hurst Castle (or Block House rather) erected by order of King Henry VIII upon a spot of earth a good way into the sea, and joined to the firm land by a narrow neck of sand which is covered over with small loose stones and pebbles, and upon both sides the sea beats, so as at spring tides and stormy weather the land passage is formidable and hazardous. The Castle has very thick stone walls, and the platforms are regular, and both have several culverines and sakers* mounted, which if their shot doth not reach such ships as pass that narrow strait that is much frequented, they threaten them; nevertheless a dismal receptacle or place for so great a Monarch, the greatest part of whose life and reign had been prosperous and full of earthly glory. But by his example, we are taught that greatest persons many times meet with adverse changes, and are forced to bow under the strokes of misfortune, yea, in their highest exaltation, are the usual marks at which the instruments of envy and malice are levelled. So we see plainly, there is no state of man's life so happy as hath not some cross, evidencing the uncertainty of worldly enjoyments, and that real comforts are elsewhere to be expected.

The Captain of this wretched place was not unsuitable; for

*A type of cannon.

52

at the King's going ashore, he stood ready to receive him with small observance: his look was stern, his hair and large beard were black and bushy; he held a partizan* in his hand, and (*Switz*-like) had a great basket hilt sword by his side; hardly could one see a man of a more grim aspect, and no less robust and rude was his behaviour. Some of his Majesty's servants were not a little fearful of him; and that he was designed for mischief, especially when he vapoured,† being elevated with his command, and puffed up by having so Royal a Prisoner, so as probably he conceived he was nothing inferior to the Governor of the Castle at Milan. But being complained of to his superior officer, appeared a bubble; for being pretty sharply admonished, he quickly became mild and calm, a posture ill-becoming such a rhodomont, and made it visible that this humour (or tumour rather) was acted to curry favour, wherein also he was mistaken. For to give the Lieutenant-Colonel his due, after his Majesty came under his custody, he was very civil to the King, both in his language and behaviour, and courteous to those that attended upon all occasions; nor was his disposition rugged toward such as in loyalty and love came to see the King, and to pray for him; as sundry out of Hampshire did, and the neighbouring counties.

His Majesty (as it may well be granted) was very slenderly accommodated at this place. The Room he usually eat in, was neither large nor lightsome; at Noon-day (in that winter season) requiring candles; and at night he had his wax lamp set (as formerly) in a silver bason, which illuminated his Bed-chamber. This sad condition makes me call to mind a relation you‡ once imparted to me well worth the remembrance, that

*A long-handled spear. Also used to describe soldiers armed with this weapon.
†Boasted.
‡Sir William Dugdale, antiquarian, to whom the memoirs were originally written.

the late Earl of Lindsey (being one of the Gentlemen of his Majesty's Bedchamber) one night lying on a pallate* by the King's Bedchamber (not long before his leaving Oxford, and going thence to the Scots) at the foot thereof (as was usual every night) was placed a lamp, or round cake of wax in a silver bason set upon a stool; the Earl awaking in the night, observed the room to be perfectly dark and thereupon raising himself up, looked towards the lamp, and concluded that it might be extinguished by some water got into the bason by some creek; but not hearing the King stir, he forebore rising, or to call upon those that lay in the next Chamber to bring in another light, fearing to disturb the King's rest; and about an hour after he fell asleep again, and awakened not till morning; but when he did awake, he discerned the lamp bright burning, which so astonished him, that taking the boldness to call to the King (whome he heard by his stirring to be awake) he told him what he had observed; whereupon the King replied that he himself awaking also in the night, took notice that all was dark; and to be fully satisfied, he put by the curtain to look at the lamp; but some time after he found it light, and concluded the Earl was risen, and had set it upon the bason lighted again. The Earl assured his Majesty he did not. The King then said he did consider it as a prognostic of God's future favour and mercy towards him or his; that although he was at that time so eclipsed, yet either he or they might shine out bright again. To return.

In this ecliptic condition was the King (the place and military persons duly considered) sequestered in a manner from the comfort earth and air affords; and in some sort from the society of men; the earth confining his Majesty to that promontory or gravel walk overspread with loose stones a good depth, which rendered it very uneasy and offensive to

*Pallet, a straw bed or mattress.

54

his feet; but endured it with his accustomed patience and serenity of spirit, and with more alacrity than they that followed him.

The air was equally noxious, by reason of the marish grounds that were about, and the unwholesome vapours arising from the sargasso's and weeds, the salt water constantly at tides and storms cast upon the shore, and by the fogs that those marine places are most subject to; so as the dwellers thereabouts find by experience, how that the air is insalubrious, and disposing to diseases, especially aguish distempers. Nevertheless, in this dolorous place the King was content to walk above two miles in length, but a few paces in breadth; the Governor one time, Captain Reynolds at another, discoursing, and Mr Harrington or Mr Herbert, by his Majesty's order, and their duty, ever attending him. That which made some amends, was a fair and uninterrupted prospect a good way into the sea, a view into the Isle of Wight one way and main land the other, with the sight of ships of all sizes daily under sail, with which his Majesty was much delighted.

During his Majesty's confinement at Hurst Castle, it so happened, that Mr Harrington, being one morning in company with the Governor and some other officers of the Army, he fell into some discourse with them concerning the late Treaty at Newport, wherein he magnified the King's Wisdom in his arguments with the Commissioners upon the propositions and satisfaction the Parliament had in his concessions, and probability of a happy event, if this force in removing him had not intervened, and made an unhappy fracture, which created parties; enlarging upon his Majesty's learned disputes with Mr Vines, and the other Presbyterian divines, with such moderation, as gained applause from all those that heard them argue: which discourse, how inoffensive soever, and without exception, at any other time and place, it appears that truth is not at all times seasonable nor safe to be spoken, as by Mr Harrington's example was evidenced; for those captious persons with whom he held discourse, being full of jealousies, and apt to wrest his words to the worst sense, they withdrew a little, and at their return told him plainly, they were dissatisfied with what he had said. He prayed them to instance wherein. They replied that in all particulars; which when he began to repeat for his own justification and their better understanding, they interrupted him, and told him in plain terms, they could not suffer his attendance any longer about the King. Which proceeding and dismiss without acquainting him with the occasion, was ill resented by the King, who had Mr Harrington in his good esteem, being a gentleman qualified with special parts, and having found him trusty, his service was the more acceptable; but blamed him nevertheless for not being more wary amongst men, that at such a time were full of jealousies, and very little obliging to his Majesty.

There was none now left to wait upon the King in his Bedchamber but Mr Herbert, and he *in motu trepidationis*,* who, nevertheless held out, by his careful observing his Majesty's instructions, without which (as the times then were) it had been impossible for him to have kept his station.

His Majesty being thus reduced to this deplorable condition, he could not choose but have some melancholy apprehensions, and accordingly about midnight there was an unusual noise, that awakened the King out of his sleep, and was in some marvel to hear the drawbridge let down at that unseasonable hour, and some horse men enter, who being alighted, the rest of that night was in deep silence. The King being desirous to know the matter, he before break of day

*In fear and trembling.

rung his silver bell, which, with both his watches, were usually laid upon a stool near the wax lamp, that was set near them in a large silver bason; upon which call, Mr Herbert opened the Bedchamber door, to know his Majesty's pleasure. The King told him, he would rise; and as he was making ready, he asked him, if he heard the noise that was about midnight; Mr Herbert answered that he did, as also the falling of the drawbridge; but being shut up in the back stair room, by the Governor's order being bolted without, he neither could nor would, without his Majesty's order, adventure out at such a time of night. The King then bad him go and learn what the matter was; and accordingly Mr Herbert went, and knocking at the back-stair door, the soldiers unbolted it without, and he within, and entering into the next room, he happily found Captain Reynolds there alone by a fire; and after some discourse, he enquired of the Captain, who they were that came so very late into the Castle, and their errand? The Captain, in a joking way, bad him be wary in carrying news to the King, he was amongst suspicious superintendants, and his comrade served for his example. Mr Herbert thanked him for his friendly caution, and at length got out of him who the commander was that came so late into the Castle, but would not discover what his business was.

Mr Herbert speedily returning to his Majesty, told him, it was Major Harrison that came so late into the Castle. 'Are you sure it was Major Harrison?' said the King. 'May it please your Majesty,' said Mr Herbert, 'Captain Reynolds told me so.' 'Then I believe it,' said the King; 'but did you see Major Harrison?' 'No, Sir,' said Mr Herbert. 'Would not Captain Reynolds,' saith the King, 'tell you what the Major's business is?' Mr Herbert replied he did what he could to be informed, but all he could then learn from the

Captain was, the occasion of Harrison's coming would be known speedily. The King said no more, but bad him attend in the next room, and went to prayer. In less than an hour the King opened the Bedchamber door, and beckoned to Mr Herbert to come in and make him ready. Mr Herbert was in some consternation to see his Majesty so much discomposed, and wept; which the King observing, asked him the meaning of it? Mr Herbert replied, 'Because I perceive your Majesty so much troubled and concerned at the news I brought.' 'I am not afraid,' said the King, 'but do not you know that this is the man who intended to assassinate me, as by letter I was informed, during the late Treaty. To my knowledge I never saw the Major, though I have heard oft of him, nor ever did him injury. The Commissioners, indeed, hearing of it, represented it from Newport to the House of Lords; what satisfaction he gave them I cannot tell; this I can, that I trust in God, who is my Helper, I would not be surprised; this is a place fit for such a purpose. Herbert, I trust to your care; go again, and make further enquiry into his business.' Mr Herbert immediately went out, and finding an opportunity to speak in private with Captain Reynolds, (who being a gentleman well educated, and at all essays expressed civility towards the King, with whom he most times walked on the stony ground, formerly mentioned, and was courteous to his servants) he told him, that the Major's business was to remove the King thence to Windsor Castle within three days at the farthest. Mr Herbert believing that the King would be well pleased with the exchange, by leaving the worst to enjoy the best Castle in England, returned to his Majesty with a mirthful countenance, little imagining (God knows) the sad consequence. And as soon as the King heard Windsor named, he seemed to rejoice at it.

Major Harrison stayed two nights at Hurst; and when it

was dark (having given orders for the King's removal) he returned from whence he came, without seeing the King, or speaking with any that attended his Majesty.

Two days after, Lieutenant-Colonel Cobbet came and acquainted his Majesty with the orders he had received for his remove thence to Windsor Castle forthwith. The King told him he was more kind now than he was at Newport, when he would not gratify him or any other with the knowledge of the place he was to go to. Windsor was a place he ever delighted in, and would make amends for what at Hurst he had suffered.

All things being, in short time made ready, he bad solitary Hurst adieu; and having passed the narrow passage (which reaches well nigh from Hurst to Milford, three long miles) there appeared a party of horse belonging to that Army, and had then their winter quarter at Lind-Hurst, and were ordered to convoy the King to Winchester; but going first to Ringwood, then through the New Forest to Rumsey (where is a fair Church, being the remains of a dissolved Nunnery, founded by great King Edgar, about the year of our Lord, 970,) went from thence to the City of Winchester, which was heretofore the Royal Seat of the West Saxon Kings, the bones of many of them being shrined in little gilded coffers, by Bishop Fox, and placed upon the top of some walls within the Choir of the Cathedral, first built by Kinelwalch a West Saxon King, upon the subversion of a Monastery of Monks, which, during the Roman Empire flourished; but that decaying, it was with greater magnificence re-edified by succeeding Bishops, since the Conquest, and all the West part by Bishop Wickham from the Choir. And amongst other famous prelates here born, were Saint Swithin, Bishop of this See, *Anno Dom.* 840 and William (the son of Herbert, who was Lord Chamberlain to King Henry I) made Archbishop of York, by

King Stephen, *Anno Dom.* 1145 and canonized in the Year of our Lord 1226 by Honorius the Pope.

At the King's Entrance into Winchester, the Mayor and Aldermen of the City (notwithstanding the times) received the King with dutiful respect, and the Clergy did the like; yea, during his short stay there, the gentry, and others of inferior rank, flocked thither in great numbers to welcome his Majesty; some out of curiousity to see, others out of zeal to pray for his enlargement and happiness; with which the King was much satisfied, and was pleased to many of them to give his hand to kiss. Thence his Majesty rode to Alresford, and then to Alton;* the inhabitants round about making haste to see his Majesty pass by, and with joyful acclamations accompanying him likewise with prayers for his preservation, a sure evidence of affection. From Alton the King passed to Farnham, betwixt which two towns (being about seven miles asunder) another troop of horse was in good order drawn up, by which his Majesty passed: It was to bring up the rear. In the head of it was the Captain gallantly mounted and armed; a velvet monteir† was on his head, a new buff coat upon his back, and a crimson silk scarf about his waist richly fringed; who as the King passed by with an easy pace (as delighted to see men well horsed and armed) the Captain gave the King a bow with his head, all *a-Soldade*,‡ which his Majesty requited. This was the first time the King saw that Captain.

Mr Herbert riding a little behind the King (who made no use of his coach since he came from Hurst Castle) he called him to come near, and asked him who the Captain was; and being told it was Major Harrison, the King viewed him more narrowly, and fixed his eyes so steadily upon him as made the

*Herbert originally put the route as Winchester–Alton–Al(r)esford–Farnham, which is obviously impossible.

†A kind of cap with a spherical crown and a flap to cover the ears.

‡In a military manner.

Major abashed, and fall back to his troop sooner than probably he intended. The King said, 'He looked like a soldier,
and that his aspect was good, and found him not such a one
as was represented; and that having some judgment in faces,
if he had observed him so well before, he should not have
harboured that ill opinion of him; for oft-times the spirit and
disposition may be discerned by the countenance; yet in that
one may be deceived.'

That night the King got to Farnham, where he was lodged
in a private gentleman's house in the Town. The Castle is
upon the ascent, and belongs to the Bishop of Winchester;
but being then a garrison, was no fit place for the King's
accommodation; nor was the Bishop there, or at that time in
a condition to pay his observance (as in duty he otherwise
would) unto his Majesty.

A little before supper, his Majesty standing by the fire in a
large parlour wainscoted, and in discourse with the mistress
of the house, the King (albeit the room was pretty full of
Army officers, and country people that crowded in to have a
sight of the King) nevertheless discovered Major Harrison at
the far end of the room talking with another officer; the King
beckoned to him with his hand to come nearer him; which he
did with due reverence. The King then taking him by his
arm, drew him aside towards the window, where, for half an
hour, or more they discoursed together; and amongst other
things, the King minded him of the information concerning
him, which if true, rendered him an enemy in the worst sense
to his person; to which the Major in his vindication assured
his Majesty, that what was so reported of him was not true;
what he had said, he might repeat, that the law was equally
obliging to great and small, and that justice had no respect to
persons; or words to that purpose; which his Majesty finding
affectedly spoken, and to no good end, he left off further

communication with him, and went to supper, being all the time very pleasant, which was no small rejoicing to many there, to see him so cheerful in that company, and such a condition.

Next day the King rode from Farnham, to Bagshot, where, at the Lord Newburgh's house, he dined; and so through part of the Forest to Windsor Castle; his usual Bedchamber in the Palace, towards the far end of the Castle Ward, being prepared for him.

Colonel Whitchcott was at that time Governor of the Castle, which was then garrisoned with some foot Companies. Here the King seemed to take more delight than at any place he had been since his leaving Hampton Court. Here he had the liberty to walk where and when he pleased, within the Castle, and in the long terrace, without, that looks towards the fair College of Eton. This terrace is of great length, upon the north side of that most magnificent structure. It was begun by Queen Elizabeth, and enlarged by succeeding Princes. And albeit you have a larger prospect from the Keep; yet from the terrace you have also a delightful view of the River of Thames, of many pleasant hills and valleys, villages and fair houses, far and near; so as no place in this Kingdom may compare with it, save the little Castle or Lodge in Greenwich Park, which has the sight of the great and noble City of London, River of Thames, and ships of great burthen daily under sail passing to and fro; with other things enumerated by Barclay in his *Argenis*.* The greatest part of the forenoon the King spent in prayer and other exercises of piety; part of the afternoon he set apart for health, by recreating himself in walking, and usually in the long terrace. The Governor here, as in other places (after the commissioners were gone) was for the most part in his company,

*A popular romance written in Latin by John Barclay (1582–1621).

for want of others to discourse with. None of the nobility, nor few of the gentry, were suffered to come into the Castle to see the King, save upon the Sundays to sermon in St George's Chapel, where the Chaplain to the Governor and garrison preached. Colonel Whitchcott behaved himself nevertheless very civilly towards the King, and his observance was taken notice of by his Majesty; as also the soldiers there, who, in their places, gave no offence either in language or behaviour to the King, or any that served him.

Whilst his Majesty stayed at Windsor, little passed worth the taking notice of; notwithstanding, some thing may be remembered: One night, as the King was preparing to go to bed, as his custom was, he wound up both his watches, one being gold, the other silver, he missed his diamond Seal, a table that had the King's Arms cut with great curiosity, and fixed to the watch; matter and work were both of considerable value. The Seal was set in a collet of gold, fastened to a gold chain. His Majesty could not imagine either when or where it dropped out; but thought he had it the day before when he looked upon his watch, as he walked in the long terrace, which being the most probable place to find it in, he bade Mr Herbert look there the next morning; which, so soon as the King was ready, and had given him his George and Garter (which his Majesty never failed to wear) the King went to his devotion, and his servant to search for the diamond, and for near an hour's space walked upon the terrace, casting his eye everywhere, but could not find it. Some officers of the garrison were then upon the terrace, who observed how intent he was; so as they imagined he had lost something, and were inquisitive to know what it was; but, he, apprehending the danger in telling them, and hazard it would run if they should find it, let them know nothing concerning it. He in like manner sought in the presence, privy chamber, galleries, St George's Hall, and every room the King had been in; but all to no purpose. So as with an anxious look he returned with this account, that he had diligently searched everywhere in likely places, and could not find it, and to acquaint any other he durst not (in regard his Majesty's Arms were engraved in it) unless his Majesty had so directed. The King perceiving Mr Herbert troubled at this accident, bid him not vex himself about it.

Next night, a little before his Majesty went to bed, a good charcoal fire being in the chamber, and wax lights burning, the King cast his eye to one end of the room, and saw something sparkle, and pointing with his finger, bade Mr Herbert take a candle and see what it was; by good providence it was the diamond, which he took up, and found his Majesty's Arms in it, and with joy brought it to the King. Another night his Majesty appointed Mr Herbert to come into his Bedchamber an hour sooner than usual in the morning; but it so happened, that he overslept his time, and awakened not until the King's silver bell hastened him in. 'Herbert (said the King), you have not observed the command I gave last night.' He acknowledged his fault. 'Well (said the King), I will order you for the future; you shall have a gold alarm watch, which, as there may be cause, shall awake you; write to the Earl of Pembroke to send me such a one presently.' The Earl immediately sent to Mr East, his watchmaker in Fleet Street, about it; of which more will be said at his Majesty's coming to St James's.

Another accident happened about this time, which might have proved of ill consequence, if God in mercy had not prevented it. Mr Herbert lodged in a little back room near the Bedchamber, towards Eton College; it had a back stair, but was at this time rammed up with earth, to prevent any passage that way. In this room he had a pallat, which (for the

SIR THOMAS HERBERT

weather was very sharp) he laid somewhat too near the chimney, and there were two baskets filled with charcoal, for the use of his Majesty's Bedchamber; and being asleep in bed, a basket took fire, either from some spark of the charcoal on the hearth, or some other way he knew not of; but the room was soon hot, and the fire got to the pallat bed, which quickly roused Mr Herbert out of sleep, who, in amazement ran to the King's Chamber door, and in a frightful manner, with that noise, awakened the King. Those in the ante-chamber without, being soldiers, hearing the King's Chamber was on fire, desired entrance (for the door was bolted within, as the King ordered) pretending that they might help to quench it; but through the goodness of God, without other assistance, those within suppressed it, by stifling it with clothes and confining it to the chimney, which was spacious. Mr Herbert humbly begged his Majesty's pardon for the disturbance he gave, not knowing how to help it. The King said, he did but his duty.

Soon after this, the Governor acquainted his Majesty, he understood how that within few days he was to be removed thence to Whitehall. To this his Majesty made little reply; seeming nothing so delighted with this remove, as he was with the former; but turning him about said, 'God is everywhere alike in Wisdom, Power and Goodness.'

Some information he had, how preposterously things went in both Houses of Parliament, wherein he was concerned; and how that the Army officers had then published a Remonstrance,* designing thereby an alteration of the Government, and trial of his person by some way that was extra-

---

*Drawn up by the army in November 1648. It called for negotiations with the King to be broken off, for a new Parliament 'freely chosen' by the people and for the trial of the King on the charge of trying to convert a limited into an absolute monarchy.

ordinary and unprecedented; so that immediately he retired into his Bedchamber, and was a good while private in his addresses to God, ever having recourse to Him by prayer and meditation, in what condition soever he was, as being the surest way to find comfort.

PART II

THE TRIAL

John Rushworth's Account

MONDAY, DECEMBER 4 1648

This day the House of Commons according to former Order further debated his Majesty's concessions, whether satisfactory or not, about which they spent all Friday and Saturday last week, and not one vote past, and the question in no way likely to be decided this day.

TUESDAY, DECEMBER 5 1648

This morning early, the House having sat all night, the question was put and voted, that his Majesty's concessions to the propositions of Parliament upon the Treaty* are sufficient grounds for settling the Peace of the Kingdom.†

MONDAY, DECEMBER 25 1648

A petition was this day presented to the House of Commons, in the name of the inhabitants of the County of Norfolk, and very gratefully accepted, the Petition was as follows.

'To the Honourable the Commons of England assembled in Parliament.

'The Humble Petition of the well affected gentlemen and others the inhabitants of the County of Norfolk and County of the City of Norwich,

---

*The negotiations at Newport. See p. 43.
†On December 6 Pride's Purge took place and from then on, what remained of Parliament was in closer agreement with the army officers.

'Humbly Sheweth,

'That after a vast expense of Blood and Treasure for many years continuance, we have expected a firmer establishment of our native liberties, but by the just hand of God upon us for our old and new Provocations in our unchristian Divisions, and abominable self-seeking that is amongst us, even of all conditions, and through the restless malice of our secret and open adversaries, we are under the shadows of hope cast back into as great fears and dangers as ever, having no greater security against our former evils than at first, if so much. Now to the end we may not deliver ourselves to ruin by neglecting of our first Principles, sealed with Oaths, Vows and Covenants, as well as the naturalities of Sense and Reason, assuring common and public, if not universal good hereby, We humbly offer these following Offers to the Honourable House for the redress of present, and prevention of future evils.

'Viz. That present inquiry be made, who have been the chief instruments of the King in the former or this latter War, and the late inviting and bringing in the Scots, and that he himself and all such as have been the most notorious incendiaries and instruments in shedding blood, may without further delay be brought to due and impartial justice, the remissness in which upon serious inquisition we fear to be one of the chiefest causes of God's so great displeasure in the several judgments now on this Nation. . . .'

THURSDAY, DECEMBER 28 1648

The Committee appointed to consider of the drawing up of a charge and the manner of the Trial of his Majesty, reported an Ordinance this day to the House for attainting him of High Treason, and for trying him by such Commissioners as should be nominated in the Body of the said Ordinance. The

House having read it the first time, ordered it to be read the second time tomorrow morning at 10 o'clock. The Charge runs thus:

'That Charles Stuart hath acted contrary to his Trust, in departing from the Parliament, setting up his Standard, making a War against them, and thereby been the occasion of much bloodshed and misery to the people whom he was set over for good. That he gave Commissions to Irish Rebels, and since was the occasion of a second War, besides what he has done contrary to the liberties of the subject, and tending to the destruction of the Fundamental Laws and Liberties of this Kingdom.'

FRIDAY, DECEMBER 29 1648

The House according to former Order proceeded in the reading of the Ordinance for impeaching of Charles Stuart of High Treason the second time in debate thereof, and ordered that the said Ordinance should be committed to a Committee to be chosen for that purpose to consider thereof, and report the same to the House with all speed.

SATURDAY, DECEMBER 30 1648

The House again had reported to them the Ordinance of Attainder and Charge against the King, in the Name of Charles Stuart, for High Treason, and ordered that the same should be committed to the former Committee chosen for that business, who were to meet this afternoon, and insert the names of such Commissioners as should be appointed by the said Ordinance for the Trial of him. They were likewise to make some special provision in case the King should refuse to plead to the Charge against him, and were to make report of the whole business on Monday morning next.

MONDAY, JANUARY I 1649

This day the Commons had again reported to them the ordinance of Attainder against the King, in the name of Charles Stuart, and the names of such commissioners as should try him, consisting of Lords, Commons, Officers of the Army, Aldermen, and other Commanders of the City, with some gentlemen from the Counties, all of them consisting of one hundred and fifty, and twenty of them are to be a Committee for the Trial of him, and to give sentence against him. By this Ordinance the Commissioners are limited to a months time to make a full determination of the business. The place of trial is not named in the Ordinance, so that whether it will be at Windsor or Westminster is not yet known. The Ordinance is to be sent tomorrow to the House of Lords for their concurrence. And to confirm the present trial and foundation thereof, and prevention of the like for the future, the House declared:

'That the Lords and Commons assembled in Parliament, do declare and adjudge, that, by the Fundamental Laws of this Realm, it is Treason in the King of England for the time to come to levy War against the Parliament and Kingdom of England.'

AN ACT OF THE COMMONS OF ENGLAND ASSEMBLED IN PARLIAMENT FOR ERECTING A HIGH COURT OF JUSTICE FOR TRYING AND JUDGING OF CHARLES STUART KING OF ENGLAND

'Whereas it is notorious, That Charles Stuart, the now King of England, not content with those many encroachments which his predecessors had made upon the people in their Rights and Freedoms, hath had a wicked design totally to subvert the ancient and fundamental Laws and Liberties of this Nation, and in their Trade to introduce an Arbitrary and Tyrannical Government, and that besides all other evil Ways and Means to bring this design to pass, he hath prosecuted it with fire and sword levyed, and maintained a cruel War in the Land against the Parliament and Kingdom, whereby the Country has been miserably wasted, the public treasure exhausted, trade decayed, thousands of people murdered, and infinite other mischiefs committed for all which high and treasonable offences the said Charles Stuart might long since justly have been brought to exemplary and condign punishment. Whereas also the Parliament, well hoping that the restraint and imprisonment of his person, after it had pleased God to deliver him into their hands, would have quieted the distempers of the Kingdom, did forbear to proceed judicially against him, but found by sad experience, that their remissness served only to encourage him and his complices in the continuance of their evil practices, and in raising of new commotions, rebellions and invasions. For prevention therefore of the like or greater inconveniences, and to the end no chief Officer or Magistrate whatsoever, may hereafter presume Traitorously and maliciously to imagine or contrive the enslaving or destroying of the English Nation and to expect impunity for so doing: Be it ordained and enacted by the Commons in Parliament, and it is hereby ordained and enacted by the Authority thereof, That [the following persons]* shall be and are hereby appointed and required to be Commissioners and Judges for the hearing, trying and adjudging of the said Charles Stuart and the said Commissioners or any twenty or more of them, shall be and are hereby authorised and constituted an High Court of Justice, to meet and sit at such convenient time and place, as by the said

*Rushworth here includes the names of the 150 members of the Court starting with Fairfax, Cromwell and Ireton.

Commissioners or the major part of twenty or more of them under their hands and seals shall be appointed and notified by public proclamation in the great Hall or Palace Yard at Westminster, and to adjourn from time to time, and from place to place, as the said High Court or major part thereof meeting shall hold fit, and to take order for the charging of him the said Charles Stuart with the crimes and treasons above mentioned, and for the receiving of his personal answer thereunto, and for the examination of witnesses upon oath, which the court hath hereby authority to administer, or otherwise, and taking any other evidence concerning the same, and thereupon, or in default of such answer, to proceed to final sentence, according to justice and the merit of the cause, and such final sentence to execute or cause to be executed speedily and impartially. And the said Court is hereby authorised and required to appoint and direct all such Officers, Attendants, and other Circumstances as they or the major part of them shall in any sort judge necessary or useful for the orderly and good managing of the premises. And Thomas Lord Fairfax the General, and all Officers and Soldiers under his command, and all officers of Justice and other well affected persons, are hereby authorised and required to be aiding and assisting unto the said Court in the due execution of the Trust hereby committed. Provided that this Act and the Authority hereby granted, do continue in force for the space of one month from the making hereof, and no longer.'

TUESDAY, JANUARY 2 1649

The Ordinance for trial of the King was by message this day carried up to the Lords for their concurrence. There sat many more Lords this day in the House than usual of late, as the Earl of Northumberland, Earl of Manchester, Earl of

Rutland, Lords North, Rochford, Maynard, Dacres, in all sixteen, the Earl of Denbigh Speaker. The Lords read the Ordinance, but stuck much upon the declaratory vote. At last they agreed as to a present answer to the Commons, that they would send answer by messengers of their own, and laying aside the business adjourned until Thursday come sevennight.*

WEDNESDAY, JANUARY 3 1649

The House of Commons taking notice that the Lords had ejected their Ordinance for trial of the King, and adjourned for a week, they first passed instructions for some of their members to go up to examine the Lords Journal book concerning their declaration and Ordinance that was the day before sent up for Trial of the King. At their return they brought to the House three Votes which their Lordships had made: 1. To send answer by messengers of their own. 2. That their Lordships do not concur to the Declaration. 3. That their Lordships rejected the Ordinance for the Trial of the King.

Hereupon the Commons voted, that all members of the House of Commons and others appointed by Order of that House, or Ordinance of both Houses of Parliament, to act in any Ordinance wherein the Lords are joined, be empowered and enjoined to sit, act, and execute in the said several Committees of themselves, notwithstanding the House of Peers join not with them herein.

*The speech of the Earl of Northumberland is particularly striking as reflecting the mood of the House. 'Not one in twenty of the people in England,' he said, 'are yet satisfied whether the King did levy war against the Houses first, or the Houses first against him; and, besides, if the King did levy war first, we have no law extant that can be produced to make it treason in him to do; and, for us, my Lords, to declare treason by an ordinance, when the matter of fact is not yet proved, nor any law to bring to judge it by, seems to me to be very unreasonable.'

They then also ordered an Expedient to be brought concerning the King, the substance like the former Ordinance for his Trial, with the foregoing Declaration intended for both Houses, now to be by the Commons only, the Committee to sit presently, and to report it this afternoon. During the time of that Committee's sitting the House adjourned.

Afterwards the House sat again, and the Ordinance was reported by the said Committee according to the instructions which were made, and recommitted back again to the said Committee, and ordered to be brought in again the next day.

THURSDAY, JANUARY 4 1649

The House this day, as was appointed, had the Ordinance for the Trial of the King by the name of Charles Stuart, reported with some amendments. And in respect of the House of Lords having rejected it, they ordered the House should be turned into a grand Committee to consider of the Power of the Commons of England when assembled in Parliament. In fine, the Committee came to this resolution, that it should be reported to the House these Votes following as the opinion of the said Committee:

'That the Commons of England assembled in Parliament do declare, that the People under God are the original of all just Power.

'They do likewise declare that the Commons of England assembled in Parliament, being chosen by, and representing the People, have the supreme Authority of this Nation.*

'They do likewise declare, that whatsoever is enacted and declared Law by the Commons of England assembled in Parliament, hath the force of Law, and all the people of this

*The Commons was, of course, only a small fraction of the original House, and even the full House was elected, on a restricted property franchise, by a minority of the population.

Nation are included thereby, although the consent and concurrence of the King and House of Peers be not had thereunto.'

These being reported to the House, the House put them
one after another to the question, and there was not one
Negative Voice to any one of them. Then the Ordinance for
Trial of Charles Stuart was again read and assented unto,
and ordered to be forthwith ingrossed in Parchment, and to
be brought in tomorrow morning.

The House ordered that the Clerk of that House should be
enjoined not to give out any Copy of the said Ordinance for
Trial of Charles Stuart, either to any Member of the House,
or any other whatsoever.

SATURDAY, JANUARY 6 1649

The Ordinance of Parliament for trying of the King was this
day brought in fairly ingrossed in parchment according to
former Order, and was read and assented to; the manner of
his Trial as before, the time and place whether at London or
Windsor, nothing further, but that is left to the Commissioners who are to try him. They are to meet on Monday
next in the Painted Chamber, Westminster, and to proceed in
order as to the Trial, which they are to go on withal without
intermission.

A letter came from the Committee of Estates in Scotland
resident here, laying open and pressing much for Unity of
Councils and Actions, according to the Covenants betwixt
the two Kingdoms, desiring that the House would not proceed to try or execute the King till the advice of that Nation
be had thereunto.

The Scots letter was not read, but ordered to be considered
of another time. The House had much debate concerning
Proceedings of Law, the issuing of Writs, and the like, in what

name they should now be made, in relation that King and Lords are laid aside.

The House referred it to a Committee to draw up an Expedient, and report to the House with speed.

TUESDAY, JANUARY 9 1649

Their Lordships had in debate their last Votes about trial of the King, and that something should be published to satisfy upon what grounds they rejected the Commission for trial of the King, but came to no resolution herein. They have sat this week, but done nothing we hear of.

This morning (according to order of the Commissioners for trial of the King yesterday) Proclamation was made in Westminster Hall to give notice that the Commissioners were to sit again tomorrow, and that all who had anything to say against the King might then be heard. This Proclamation was in this manner made: Serjeant Dendy, Serjeant at Arms to the Commissioners, rode into Westminster Hall, with the Mace belonging to the House of Commons on his shoulders, and some Officers also attending him, and six Trumpeters on horseback, a Guard of Horse and Foot attending in the Palace-Yard. The Trumpeters sounded in the middle of the Hall, and the Drums beat in the Palace-Yard, and Proclamation was made as aforesaid.

The House of Commons then sitting ordered that Serjeant Dendy should forthwith make the same Proclamation about the Trial of the King, and in the same manner, at the Old Exchange, and in Cheapside, London, which was accordingly done.

The House this day had much debate what alteration of proceedings should be made in Courts of Justice, now that the King and Lords were to be laid aside, and whether all Writs should run in the name of one person (as formerly Carolus Dei Gratia, etc.) or not.

At last they came to this result; that the name of any one particular person should not be inserted as the style of any Common Writ or otherwise for the time to come, and that it should be referred to the Committee for settling proceedings in Courts of Justice to consider how and in what manner the style should be hereafter.

They likewise voted that this present Great Seal of England should be broken in pieces, and that a new one should be forthwith made; in the mean time all proceedings under the Great Seal to be good till the new one be confirmed.

They considered what should be engraven on the said New Great Seal, and ordered that the Arms of England, the Harp, and the Arms of Ireland should be engraven on one side of the said Seal.

That the inscription on that side the Seal should be 'The Great Seal of England.'

That the inscription on the other side of the said Seal where the Sculpture or Map of the Parliament is to be engraven, shall be these words: 'In the first year of freedom by God's blessing restored, 1649.'

SATURDAY, JANUARY 13 1649*

The High Court of Justice for trial of the King, sat again this day. Their sitting hitherto hath produced little more, the whole time having been spent about settling the Court, and for more orderly proceeds, and the choosing a President, Assistants, Clerks, and other Officers, the calling of their Members, and summoning such as have not appeared.

Some proceedings also in order to the Management of the Charge against the King, and this day they had in consideration the place for trial of the King, which they agreed should

*The Court met on the 10th, only forty-five members being present, and chose Serjeant Bradshaw as its President.

be Westminster Hall, and that in order thereunto the King should be removed from Windsor, and brought up hither on Monday next.

MONDAY, JANUARY 15 1649

The High Court of Justice concerning the trial of the King, sat this day, heard his Charge read, which was very long, and therefore ordered a Committee to abbreviate it, and to peruse the proofs upon the matters of fact thereof, and to report all on Wednesday next at eight o'clock in the morning. They ordered that the Parliament should be moved to put off the next Term for fourteen days longer, in respect of this trial. In order whereunto they are making the Courts of King's Bench and Chancery into one place of Judicature for the better accommodation of his Majesty and the Commissioners.

FRIDAY, JANUARY 19 1649

The High Court of Justice for Trial of the King, this day met after the rising of the House in the Painted Chamber, and heard the proof to the several Articles of Impeachment against the King, who this day was brought from Windsor to St James's, where he lodged this night.

SATURDAY, JANUARY 20 1649

After an O Yes made, and silence commanded, the Act of the Commons in Parliament for sitting of the said Court was ready and the Court was called, every Commissioner present thereupon rising to his name.

(It is to be remembered, that at this time, the Lady Fairfax, wife to the General, being above in a window, interrupted the reading of the names of the Commissioners by speaking aloud to the Court then sitting, that her husband the Lord Fairfax was not there in person, nor ever would sit

JOHN RUSHWORTH

among them, and therefore they did him wrong to name him as a sitting Commissioner.)*

[The names of the Commissioners having been read] the Court commanded the Serjeant at Arms to send for the prisoner, and thereupon Colonel Thomlinson, who had the charge of the prisoner, within a quarter of an hours space brought him, with Colonel Hacker and thirty-two Officers with partizans guarding him, to the Court, his own servants immediately attending him. Being thus brought up in the face of the Court, the Serjeant at Arms with his Mace receives him, and conducts him straight to the Bar, having a crimson velvet chair set before him. After a stern looking upon the Court and the people in the galleries on each side of him, he places himself in the chair, not at all moving his hat or otherwise showing the least respect to the Court. Presently he riseth up again and turns about, looking downwards upon the Guards placed on the left side, and on the multitude of spectators on the right side of the said great Hall, the Guard that attended him in the meantime dividing themselves on each side of the Court, and his own servants following him to the Bar.

The prisoner having again placed himself in his chair with his face towards the Court, and silence being again ordered and proclaimed, the Lord President in the name of the Court, addressed himself to the prisoner:

'Charles Stuart, King of England, the Commons of England assembled in Parliament being deeply sensible of the evils and calamities that had been brought upon this nation, and of the innocent blood that had been spilt in it, which is fixed upon you as the principal author of it, have resolved to make inquisition for this blood, and according to the debt they did owe to God, to justice, the Kingdom and themselves,

*Her actual words were: 'He has more wit than to be here.'

and according to that fundamental power that is vested, and trust reposed in them by the people (other means failing through your default) have resolved to bring you to trial and judgment, and have therefore constituted this Court of Justice before which you are now brought, where you are to hear your charge, upon which the Court will proceed according to justice.'

Hereupon Mr Cook, Solicitor for the Commonwealth, standing within the Bar, with the rest of the Counsel for the Commonwealth, on the right hand of the prisoner, offered to speak, but the prisoner having a Staff in his hand, held it up, and softly laid it upon the said Mr Cook's shoulder two or three times, bidding him hold.* Nevertheless the Lord President ordering him to go on, Mr Cook did, according to the Order of the Court to him directed, in the name and on the behalf of the People of England, exhibit a Charge of High Treason and other High Crimes, and did therewith accuse the said Charles Stuart, King of England, praying in the name and on the behalf aforesaid, that the Charge might be accordingly received and read, and due proceedings had thereupon, and accordingly preferred a Charge in writing, which being received by the Court, and delivered to the Clerk of the Court, the Lord President in the name of the Court ordered it should be read.

The King interrupted the reading of it, but the Court notwithstanding commanded the Clerk to read it, acquainting the Prisoner, that if he had anything to say after, the Court would hear him. Whereupon the Clerk read the Charge, which is as followeth:

'That the said Charles Stuart, being admitted King of

*'Also the head of his staff happened to fall off, at which he wondered; and seeing none to take it up, he stooped for it himself.' [State Trials iv. 1,074]

England, and therein trusted with a limited Power to govern by, and according to the Laws of the Land, and not otherwise, and by his Trust, Oath and Office, being obliged to use the Power committed to him for the Good and Benefit of the People, and for the Preservation of their Rights and Liberties, yet nevertheless out of a wicked design to erect and uphold in himself an unlimited and tyrannical power to rule according to his Will, and to overthrow the Rights and Liberties of the People, yea to take away and make void the foundations thereof, and of all redress and remedy of misgovernment, which by the Fundamental Constitutions of this Kingdom were reserved on the peoples behalf in the Right and Power of frequent and successive Parliaments, or National Meetings in Council, He the said Charles Stuart, for accomplishment of such his designs, and for the protecting of himself and his adherents in his and their wicked practices, to the same ends hath traitorously and maliciously levyed War against the present Parliament and the people therein represented, particularly upon or about the thirtieth day of June, in the Year of our Lord 1642, at Beverley in the County of York, and upon or about the 24th day of August in the same year, at the County of the Town of Nottingham, where and when he set up his Standard of War, and also on or about the 23rd day of October in the same year, at Edgehill* or Keynton Field in the County of Warwick, and upon or about the 30th day of November in the same year at Brentford in the County of Middlesex, and upon or about the 30th day of August in the year of our Lord 1643, at Caversham Bridge near Reading in the County of Berks, and upon or about the 30th day of October in the year last mentioned, at or near the City of Gloucester, and upon or about the 30th day of

---

*This, and the remainder of the list, refer to the more important battles of the Civil War.

November in the year last mentioned, at Newbury in the County of Berks, and upon or about the 31st day of July in the year of our Lord 1644, at Cropredy Bridge in the County of Oxon, and upon or about the 30th day of September in the last year mentioned, at Bodmin and other places near adjacent, in the County of Cornwall, and upon or about the 30th day of November in the year last mentioned at Newbury aforesaid, and upon or about the 8th day of June in the year of our Lord 1645, at the Town of Leicester, and also upon the 14th day of the same month in the same year, at Naseby-Field in the County of Northampton. At which several times and places, or most of them, and at many other places in this land, at several other times within the years aforementioned, and in the year of our Lord 1646 he the said Charles Stuart hath caused and procured many thousands of the free people of this Nation to be slain, and by divisions, parties, and insurrections within this Land, by invasions from foreign parts, endeavoured and procured by him, and by many other evil ways and means, he, the said Charles Stuart, hath not only maintained and carried on the said War both by Land and Sea, during the years beforementioned, but also hath renewed, or caused to be renewed, the said War against the Parliament and good people of this Nation in this present year 1648 in the Counties of Kent, Essex, Surrey, Sussex, Middlesex, and many other Counties and places in England and Wales, and also by Sea. And particularly he, the said Charles Stuart, hath for that purpose given commission to his Son the Prince, and others, whereby, besides multitudes of other persons, many such as were by the Parliament instructed and employed for the safety of the Nation (being by him or his Agents corrupted to the betraying of their Trust, and revolting from the Parliament) have had entertainment and commission for the continuing and renewing of War and

Hostility against the said Parliament and people as aforesaid. By which cruel and unnatural Wars, by him the said Charles Stuart, levyed, continued, and renewed as aforesaid, much innocent blood of the free people of this Nation hath been spilt, many Families have been undone, the public Treasure wasted and exhausted, Trade obstructed and miserably decayed, vast expense and damage to the Nation incurred, and many parts of this Land spoiled, some of them even to desolation. And for further prosecution of his said evil designs, He, the said Charles Stuart, doth still continue his commissions to the said Prince, and other Rebels and Revolters both English and Foreigners, and to the Earl of Ormond,* and to the Irish Rebels and Revolters associated with him, from whom further invasions upon this Land are threatened, upon the procurement, and on the behalf of the said Charles Stuart.

'All which wicked designs, Wars, and evil practices of him the said Charles Stuart, have been, and are carried on for the advancement and upholding of a personal interest of Will, Power, and pretended Prerogative to himself and his family, against the public interest, common right, liberty, justice, and peace of the people of this Nation, by and from whom he was instructed as aforesaid.

'By all which it appeareth that the said Charles Stuart hath been, and is the occasioner, author, and continuer of the said unnatural, cruel, and bloody Wars, and therein guilty of all the treasons, murders, rapines, burnings, spoils, desolations, damages, and mischiefs, to this nation, acted and committed in the said Wars, or occasioned thereby.'†

*Charles's Lord Lieutenant in Ireland.

†After the reading of the charge Bradshaw called on Charles to answer it in the name of 'the good people of England.' Lady Fairfax again intervened: 'It is a lie. Not half nor a quarter of the people of England. Oliver Cromwell is a traitor.' The guards on duty were ordered to point their guns at the gallery and Lady Fairfax was persuaded to leave.

The King smiled at the reading of his Charge, and after reading of it, demanded of the Lord President by what lawful authority he was brought thither. Being answered, In the name of the Commons of England, He replied, he saw no Lords there, which should make a Parliament, including the King, and urged, That the Kingdom of England was hereditary and not successive, and that he should betray his Trust if he acknowledged or answered to them, for that he was not convinced they were a lawful authority. So that after he had been often commanded to answer, and refused, he was remanded to Sir Robert Cotton's house, and afterwards removed back to St James's, where he lay this night, and the Court adjourned till Monday 10 o'clock in the forenoon, further to consider of this business.

On Sunday great concourse of people went out of London to Westminster, but if to see the King, they were disappointed, who was then at St James's under a strong Guard. A solemn fast was kept at Whitehall this day by the Commissioners for trial of the King.

MONDAY, JANUARY 22 1649

This day the Commissioners from the Kingdom of Scotland delivered in to the House of Commons some papers, and a Declaration from the Parliament of Scotland, wherein they express a dislike of the present proceedings about the trial of the King, and declare that the Kingdom of Scotland has an undoubted interest in the person of the King, who was not (they say) delivered to the English Commissioners at Newcastle* for the ruin of his person, but for a more speedy settlement of the peace of his Kingdoms. That they extremely dissent and declare against the trial of him, and that this

*Charles had surrendered himself to the Scots in 1646 and they had handed him over to the care of the English Parliament.

present way of proceeding against him leaves a deep impression on them, and sits heavy on all their spirits, in regard of the great miseries that are like to ensue upon these Kingdoms.

The Scots Commissioners by their papers further moved the House that they might have leave to make their personal addresses to the King.

The House upon reading the whole referred it to a Committee to draw up an answer to the Parliament of Scotland.

This day the High Court of Justice for trial of the King sat again in Westminster Hall.

The Court being sat, O Yes made, and silence commanded, the King was sent for, whereupon Mr Solicitor Cook moved the Court, That whereas he had at the last Court in the behalf of the Commons of England exhibited a Charge of High Treason, and other high Crimes, against the prisoner at the Bar, whereof he stands accused in the name of the people of England, and the charge was ready and his answer required, he was not then pleased to give answer, but instead of answering, did there dispute the Authority of this High Court, his humble motion was, that the prisoner may be directed to make a positive answer, either by way of confession or negation, which if he shall refuse to do, that the matter of charge may be taken *pro confesso*, and the Court may proceed according to Justice.

The Lord President 'Sir, you may remember at the last Court you were told the occasion of your being brought hither, and you heard a Charge read against you, containing a Charge of High Treason, and other High Crimes against this Realm of England, and instead of answering, you interrogated the Court's authority and jurisdiction. Sir, the Authority is the Commons of England in Parliament assembled, who required your answer to the Charge either by confessing or denying.'

The King 'When I was here last, it is very true I made that question. And truly if it were only my own particular case, I would have satisfied myself with the protestation I made the last time I was here, against the legality of this Court, and that a King cannot be tried by any superior jurisdiction on Earth. But it is not my case alone, it is the freedom and liberty of the people of England, and do you pretend what you will, I stand more for their liberties, for if power without Law may make laws, may alter the fundamental laws of the Kingdom, I do not know what subject he is in England that can be sure of his life or anything that he calls his own. Therefore when that I came here, I did expect particular reasons to know by what law, what authority you did proceed against me here. And therefore I am a little to seek what to say to you in this particular, because the affirmative is to be proved, the negative often is very hard to do, but since I cannot persuade you to it, I shall tell you my reasons as short as I can.

'My reasons why in conscience and duty I owe to God first, and my people next, for the preservation of their lives, liberties, and estates, I conveive I cannot answer this till I be satisfied of the legality of it. All proceedings against any man whatsoever. . . .'

The Lord President 'Sir, I must interrupt you, which I would not do, but that what you do is not agreeable to the proceedings of any Court of Justice. You are about to enter into argument and dispute concerning the authority of this Court, before whom you appear as a prisoner, and are charged as a High Delinquent. If you take upon you to dispute the authority of the Court, we may not do it, nor will any Court give way unto it. You are to submit to it. You are to give a punctual and direct answer, whether you will answer your Charge or no, and what your answer is.'

The King 'Sir, by your favour, I do not know the Forms of Law. I do know Law and Reason, though I am no Lawyer professed. But I know as much Law as any gentleman in England, and therefore (under favour) I do plead for the liberties of the people of England more than you do. And therefore if I should impose a belief upon any without reasons given for it, it were unreasonable. But I must tell you that by that reason that I have, as thus informed, I cannot yield unto it.'

The Lord President 'Sir, I must interrupt you; you may not be permitted. You speak of law and reason. It is fit there should be law and reason, and there is both against you, Sir. The vote of the Commons of England assembled in Parliament, that is the reason of the Kingdom. It is the law of the kingdom and they are these that have given you that Law according to which you should have ruled and reigned. Sir, you are not to dispute our authority; you are told it again by the Court. Sir, it will be taken notice of that you stand in contempt of the Court, and your Contempt will be recorded accordingly.'

The King 'I do not know how a King may be a delinquent; by any law that ever I heard of, all men (Delinquents or what you will) may, let me tell you, put in demurrers against any proceeding as legal. I do demand that, and demand to be heard with my reasons. If you deny that, you deny reason.'

The Lord President 'Sir, you have offered something to the Court; I shall speak something to you, the sense of the Court. Sir, neither you nor any Man are permitted to dispute that point; you are concluded, you may not demur to the jurisdiction of the Court. If you do, I must let you know they overrule your demurrer, they sit here by the authority of the Commons of England, and all your predecessors and you are responsible to them.'

The King 'I deny that. Shew me one precedent.'

The Lord President 'Sir, you ought not to interrupt while the Court is speaking to you. This point is not to be debated by you, neither will the Court permit you to do it. If you offer it by way of demur to the jurisdiction of the Court, they have considered of their jurisdiction, they do affirm their own jurisdiction.'

The King 'I say, Sir, by your favour, that the Commons of England was never a Court of judicature, I would know how they came to be so.'

The Lord President 'Sir, you are not to be permitted to go on in that speech, and these discourses.'

Then the Clerk of the Court read as follows:

'Charles Stuart King of England, You have been accused on the behalf of the people of England, of High Treason, and other high Crimes. The Court have determined that you ought to answer the same.'

The King 'I will answer the same so soon as I know by what authority you do this.'

The Lord President 'If this be all that you will say, then gentlemen you that brought the prisoner here, take charge of him back again.'

The King 'I do require that I may give in my reasons why I do not answer, and give me time for that.'

The Lord President 'Sir, it is not for prisoners to require.'

The King 'Prisoners! Sir, I am not an ordinary prisoner.'

The Lord President 'The Court has considered of their jurisdiction, and they have already affirmed their jurisdiction. If you will not answer, we will give order to record your default.'

The King 'You never heard my reasons yet.'

The Lord President 'Sir, your reasons are not to be heard against the highest jurisdiction.'

The King 'Shew me that jurisdiction, where reason is not to be heard.'

The Lord President 'Sir, we shew it you here, the Commons of England, and the next time you are brought, you will know more of the pleasure of the Court, and it may be their final determination.'

The King 'Shew me where ever the House of Commons were a Court of Judicature of that kind.'

The Lord President 'Serjeant, take away the prisoner.'

The King 'Well, Sir, remember that the King is not suffered to give in his reasons for the Liberty and Freedom of all his subjects.'

The Lord President 'Sir, you are not to have liberty to use this language. How great a friend you have been to the laws and liberties of the people, let all England and the World judge.'

The King 'Sir, under favour, it was the liberty, freedom, and laws of the subject that I ever took to defend myself with arms. I never took up arms against the people, but for the laws.'

The Lord President 'The command of the Court must be obeyed, no answer will be given to the Charge.'

The King 'Well, Sir.'

And so he was guarded forth to Sir Robert Cotton's house.

Then the Court adjourned until the next day.

TUESDAY, JANUARY 23 1649

The Commons this day had an ordinance reported for settling of the Courts of Justice, and in what way Writs should be issued for the future. That Writs out of Chancery should go in the name of the Chancellor, or Keepers of the Seal, also in other Courts, in the name of the Judge or Judges. And whereas it has been formerly charged upon malefactors, that they have acted contrary to the peace of our Sovereign Lord the King, his Crown and Dignity, it is now to be thus, against the Peace, Justice and Council of England.

This day the High Court of Justice for trial of the King sat again in Westminster Hall, seventy-three persons present. The King comes in with his guard, looks with an austere countenance upon the Court, and sits down.

Mr Cook, Solicitor General, moved the Court, that whereas the prisoner at the Bar, instead of giving answer to the charge against him, did still dispute the Authority of the Court. That as according to Law, if a Prisoner shall stand as contumacious in contempt, and shall not put in an issuable plea Guilty or not Guilty of the Charge given against him, whereby he may come to a fair trial, that by an implicit confession it may be taken *pro confesso*, as it hath been done to those who deserved more favour than the prisoner at the Bar has done, and therefore that speedy judgment be pronounced against him.

The Lord President 'Sir, You have heard what is moved by the Counsel on the behalf of the Kingdom against you. Sir, you may well remember, and if you do not, the Court cannot forget what dilatory dealings the Court has found at your hands. You were pleased to propound some questions, you had our resolutions upon them. You were told over and over again, that the Court did affirm their own jurisdiction, that it was not for you nor any other man to dispute the jurisdiction of the supreme and highest authority of England, from which there is no appeal, and touching which there must be no dispute, yet you did persist in such carriage as you gave no manner of obedience, nor did you acknowledge any authority in them, nor the High Court that constituted this Court of Justice.

'Sir, I must let you know from the Court that they are very sensible of these delays of yours, and that they ought not, being thus authorised by the Supreme Court of England, to be thus trifled withal, and that they might in justice, if they pleased, and according to the Rules of Justice, take advantage of these delays, and proceed to pronounce judgment against you, yet nevertheless they are pleased to give direction, and on their behalfs I do require you that you make a positive answer unto this Charge, that is against you, Sir, in plain terms, for justice knows no respect of persons. You are to give your positive and plain answer in plain English, whether you be guilty or not guilty of these Treasons laid to your charge.'

The King, after a little pause said:

'When I was here yesterday, I did desire to speak for the liberties of the people of England. I was interrupted. I desire to know yet whether I may speak freely or no.'

The Lord President 'Sir, you have had the resolution of the Court upon the like question the last day, and you were told that having such charge of so high a nature against you, your work was, that you ought to acknowledge the jurisdiction of the Court, and to answer to your Charge. Sir, if you answer to your Charge, which the Court gives you leave now to do, though they might have taken the advantage of your contempt, yet if you be able to answer your Charge, when you have once answered, you shall be heard at large, make the best defence you can. But, Sir, I must let you know from the Court, as their Commands, that you are not permitted to issue out into any other discourses, till such time as you have given a positive answer concerning the matter that is charged upon you.'

The King 'For the Charge, I value it not a rush. It is the liberty of the People of England I stand for. For me to acknowledge a new Court, that I never heard of before, I that am your King, that should be an example to all the people of England, to uphold justice, to maintain the old laws, indeed I do not know how to do it. You spoke very well the first day that I came here of the obligations that I had laid upon me by God, to the maintenance of the liberties of my people, the same obligation you spoke of, I do acknowledge to God that I owe to him, and to my people, to defend as much as in me lies the ancient laws of the Kingdom. Therefore, until that I may know that this is not against the fundamental Laws of the Kingdom, by your favour, I can put in no particular answer. If you will give me time, I will show you my reasons why I cannot do it, and thus. . . .'

Here being interrupted, he said:

'By your favour, you ought not to interrupt me. How I came here I know not, there's no Law for it, to make your King your prisoner. I was in a Treaty upon the public faith of the Kingdom,* that was by the known two Houses of Parliament, that was the Representative of the Kingdom, and when that I had almost made an end of the Treaty, then I was hurried away and brought hither, and therefore . . .'

The Lord President 'Sir, you must know the pleasure of the Court.'

The King 'By your Favour, Sir.'

The Lord President 'Nay, Sir, by your favour, you may not be permitted to fall into those discourses: You appear as a delinquent, you have not acknowledged the authority of the Court. The Court craves it not of you, but once more they command you to give your positive answer. Clerk, do your Duty.'

The King 'Duty, Sir!'

The Clerk reads a Paper, requiring the King to give a positive and final answer by way of confession or denial of the Charge.

*The negotiations at Newport.

The King 'Sir, I say again to you, so that I might give satisfaction to the People of England of the clearness of my proceedings, not by way of answer, not in this way, but to satisfy them, that I have done nothing against that trust that hath been committed to me. I would do it, but to acknowledge a new Court against their Privilege, to alter the fundamental Laws of the Kingdom, Sir, you must excuse me.'

The Lord President 'Sir, this is the third time that you have publicly disowned this Court, and put an affront upon it. How far you have preserved the privileges of the People, your actions have spoke it, and truly, Sir, Men's intentions ought to be known by their actions. You have written your meaning in bloody characters throughout the whole Kingdom, but, Sir, you understand the pleasure of the Court—Clerk, record the default—and Gentlemen you that took charge of the prisoner, take him back again.'

The King 'I will say this one word more to you; if it were my own particular, I would not say any more nor interrupt you.'

The Lord President 'Sir, you have heard the pleasure of the Court, and you are (notwithstanding you will not understand it) to find that you are before a Court of Justice.'

Then the King went forth with his Guard, to Sir Robert Cotton's house, where he lay the last night and this, and the Court adjourned till the next day.

WEDNESDAY, JANUARY 24 1649

This day it was expected the High Court of Justice would have met in Westminster Hall about ten of the Clock, but at the time appointed one of the Ushers by Direction of the Court (then sitting in the Painted Chamber) gave notice to the People there assembled, that in regard the Court was then upon the examination of witnesses* in relation to present affairs in the Painted Chamber, they could not sit there, but to appear upon further summons.

THURSDAY, JANUARY 25 1649

W.C. of Patrington in Holderness in the County of York, Gentleman, aged 42 years, or thereabouts, sworn and examined, saith, 'That he this deponent living at Hullbridge near Beverley, in July, 1642, did then hear that Forces were raised about 3,000 Foot, for the King's Guard, under Sir Robert Strickland.'

And this deponent further said, 'That about the 2nd of July 1642, he saw a Troop of Horse come to Beverley, being the Lord's Day, about 4 or 5 o'clock in the afternoon, called the Prince's Troop, Mr James Nelthrop being then Mayor of the said Town.'

And this deponent further said, 'That he did see that afternoon the said Troop march from Beverley aforesaid into Holderness, where they received ammunition, brought up the River of Humber unto them.'

And this deponent further said, 'That the same night being Sunday, there came about 300 Foot soldiers (said to be Sir Robert Strickland's Regiment) under the command of Lieutenant-Colonel Duncomb, and called, The King's Guard, unto this deponent's house, called Hullbridge, near Beverley, about midnight, and broke open, entered and possessed themselves of the said house, and that the Earl of Newport, the Earl of Carnarvon, and divers others came that

---

*The taking of evidence was almost certainly a device for gaining time, since no other useful purpose was served by it. The members of the court were divided among themselves, and during the next two days Cromwell and Ireton were busy persuading the fainthearted to agree to the death sentence.

THE TRIAL

night thither to the said Forces, and that the same night (as this deponent was then informed) Sir Thomas Gower, then High Sheriff of the said County came thither, and left there a warrant for staying all provisions from going to Hull to Sir John Hotham, which said warrant was then delivered to this deponent, being Constable, by Lieutenant-Colonel Duncomb.'

And this deponent further said, 'That he was by the said Forces put out of his house, and did with his family go to Beverley, and after that, viz. the Thursday following, to this deponent's best remembrance, he did see the King come to Beverley, to the Lady Gee's House there, where he this deponent did often see the King, with Prince Charles, and the Duke of York, and that the trained bands were then raised in Holderness, who were raised (as was generally reported) by the King's command.'

And this deponent further said, 'That the night after the said Forces had (as aforesaid) possessed themselves of this deponent's house, Colonel Legard's house was plundered by them, being upon a Monday, which aforesaid entry of this deponent's house was the first act of hostility that was committed in those parts.'

And this deponent further said, 'That after the said Sir Robert Strickland's said company was gone from Hullbridge, having continued there about 10 days, there then came to the said house Colonel Wivel, with about 700 foot soldiers, who then took up his quarters at Hullbridge aforesaid.' And this deponent further said, 'That the Warrant he now produces to this Court, is the same original Warrant aforesaid spoken of.'

And this deponent further said, that the General's name of the said forces that were there, and raised as aforesaid, was the Earl of Lindsey, and that this deponent was brought before him the said General, in the name of The King's Lord

General, for holding intelligence with Sir John Hotham, then Governor of Hull, and because it was then informed to the said General, that he, this deponent, had provisions of corn to send over into Ireland, which he, this deponent, was forbidden by the said General to send unto Ireland, or any place else, without his or the King's direction or Warrant first had in that behalf.

The aforesaid Warrant, mentioned in the deposition of the said W.C. is as followeth:

It is his Majesty's command, that you do not suffer any victuals or provisions of what sort soever, to be carried into the town of Hull, without his Majesty's special license first obtained, and of this you are not to fail at your peril.

Dated at Beverley, July 3 1642.

J.B. of Harwood, in the County of York, Glover, sworn and examined, said that he being a soldier under the King's command, the first day that the King's Standard was set up at Nottingham, which was about the middle of summer six years before, he this examinant did work at Nottingham, and that he did see the King within the Castle of Nottingham, within two or three days after the said Standard was so set up, and that the said Standard did fly the same day that the King was in the said Castle as aforesaid, and this deponent did hear that the King was at Nottingham the same day that the said Standard was set up, and before.

And this deponent further said, 'That there was then there the Earl of Lindsey's Regiment, who had then their Colours given them, and that the said Earl of Lindsey was then also proclaimed there, The King's General, and that it was proclaimed then there likewise in the King's name, at the Head of every Regiment, that the said Forces should fight against all that came to oppose the King, or any of his followers, and

in particular, against the Earl of Essex, the Lord Brook, and
divers others, and that they the said Earl of Essex, and Lord
Brook, and divers others, were then proclaimed Traitors, and
that the same proclamations were printed and dispersed by
the Officers of the Regiments throughout every Regiment.'

And this Deponent further said, 'That he this deponent
and the Regiment of which he then was, had their Colours
then given them, and Sir William Pennyman being the
Colonel of the said Regiment, the said Sir William Pennyman was present with his said Regiment at that time.'

And this Deponent further said, 'That the said Standard
was advanced upon the highest Tower in Nottingham Castle,
and that he this deponent did see the King often at Nottingham, at that time that the said Forces continued in Nottingham as aforesaid, they continuing there for the space of
one month, and that the drums for raising Volunteers
to fight under the King's Command, were then beaten all
the said County over, and divers other Forces were raised
there.'

And this Deponent further said, 'That he did take up
Arms under the King's Command as aforesaid, for fear of
being plundered, Sir William Pennyman giving out, that it
were a good deed to fire the said town, because they would
not go further in the King's Service, and that this deponent's
father did thereupon command him, this deponent, to take
up arms as aforesaid, and that divers others (as they did
confess) did then also take up arms for the King, for fear of
being plundered.'

And this Deponent further said, 'That in or about the
month of October 1642, he did see the King at Edgehill in
Warwickshire, where he, sitting on horse-back while his army
was drawn up before him, did speak to the Colonel of every
Regiment that passed by him, that he would have them speak

to their soldiers to encourage them to stand to it, and to fight against the Lord of Essex, the Lord Brook, Sir William Waller, and Sir William Balfour.'

And this Deponent said, 'That he did see many slain at the fight at Edgehill, and that afterwards he did see a list brought in unto Oxford, of the men which were slain in that fight, by which it was reported that there were slain 6,559 men.'

And this Deponent further said, 'Afterwards, in or about the month of November 1642, he did see the King in the head of his Army at Hounslow Heath in Middlesex, Prince Rupert then standing by him. And he this deponent, did then hear the King encourage several Regiments of Welshmen (then being in the field) which had run away at Edgehill, saying unto them, that he did hope they would regain their honour at Brentford, which they had lost at Edgehill.'*

After which the Court sat private.

The Court taking into consideration the whole matter in charge against the King, passed these Votes following, as preparatory to the Sentence against the King, but ordered that they should not be binding finally to conclude the Court.

'*Resolved* upon the whole matter, that this Court will proceed to Sentence of condemnation against Charles Stuart King of England.'

'*Resolved* that the condemnation of the King shall be for a Tyrant, Traitor and Murderer.'

'*Resolved* that the condemnation of the King, shall be likewise for being a public enemy to the commonwealth of England.'

*Twenty-nine further depositions were taken and recorded but, as they vary only in detail from the two examples quoted, they have been omitted.

'*Resolved*, that this condemnation shall extend to Death.'

The Court adjourned itself till tomorrow at one o'clock in the Afternoon.

JANUARY 26 1649

Here the Court sat private.

The draught of a sentence against the King, is according to the Votes of the 25th instant prepared, and after several Readings, Debates, and Amendments by the Court thereupon:

Resolved: That this Court do agree to the Sentence now read.

Resolved: That the said Sentence shall be ingrossed. That the King be brought to Westminster tomorrow to receive his Sentence.

The Court adjourned itself till the morrow at 10 o'clock in the morning to this place, the Court giving notice that they then intended to adjourn from thence to Westminster Hall.

JANUARY 27 1649

The sentence agreed on, and ordered by this Court the 26th instant to be ingrossed, being accordingly ingrossed, was read.

Resolved, that the Sentence now read shall be the Sentence of this Court for the condemnation of the King, which shall be read and published in Westminster Hall this day.

The Court hereupon considered of certain instructions for the Lord President to manage the business of this day in Westminster Hall, and ordered:

'That the Lord President do manage what discourse shall happen between him and the King, according to his discretion, with the advice of his two assistants, and that in case the King shall still persist in excepting against the Court's jurisdiction, to let him know that the Court do still affirm their jurisdiction.'

'That in case the King shall submit to the jurisdiction of the Court, and pray a Copy of the Charge, that then the Court do withdraw and advise.'

'That in case the King shall move anything else worth the Court's consideration, that the Lord President, upon advice of his said assistants, do give orders for the Court's withdrawing to advise.'

'That in case the King shall not submit to answer, and there happen no such cause of withdrawing, that then the Lord President do command the Sentence to be read, but that the Lord President should hear the King say what he would before the Sentence, and not after.'

And thereupon it being further moved, whether the Lord President should use any discourses or speeches to the King, as in the case of other prisoners to be condemned was usual before the publishing of the Sentence, he received general directions to do therein as he should see cause, and to press what he should conceive most seasonable and suitable to the occasion. And it was further directed, that after the reading of the Sentence, the Lord President should declare that the same was the Sentence, Judgment, and resolution of the whole Court, and that the Commissioners should thereupon signify their consent by standing up.

The Court forthwith adjourned itself to Westminster Hall.

The High Court of Justice sat in Westminster Hall.* The Lord President was in Scarlet. After the calling of the Court the King came in his wonted posture with his hat on; a cry was made in the Hall as he passed, for Justice and Execution. But silence being commanded, his Majesty began:

*Sixty-seven judges were present.

'I desire a word to be heard a little, and I hope I shall give no occasion of interruption.'

The President 'You may answer in your time, hear the Court first.'

The King 'If it please you, Sir, I desire to be heard, and I shall give no occasion of interruption, and 'tis only in a word. A sudden judgment—'

The President 'Sir, you shall be heard in due time, but you are to hear the Court first.'

The King 'Sir, I desire it, it will be in order to what I believe the Court will say, and therefore, Sir—A hasty judgment is not so soon recalled.'

The President 'Sir, you shall be heard before the Judgment be given, and in the mean time you may forbear.'

The King 'Well, Sir, shall I be heard before the Judgment be given.'

The President 'Gentlemen, It is well known to all, or most of you here present, That the Prisoner at the Bar hath been several times convented and brought before this Court, to make answer to a Charge of Treason, and other High Crimes exhibited against him in the name of the People of England. To which Charge being required to answer, he hath been so far from obeying the commands of the Court by submitting to their Justice, that he began to take upon himself to offer reasoning and debate unto the authority of the Court, and to the Highest Court that appointed them to try and judge him. But being overruled in that, and required to make his answer, he was still pleased to continue contumacious, and refuse to submit to answer. Hereupon the Court, that they might not be wanting to themselves, nor the trust reposed in them, nor that any man's wilfulness prevent justice, they have thought fit to take the matter into their consideration, they have considered of the Charge, they have considered of the contumacy, and of that concession which in Law doth arise upon that contumacy, they have likewise considered of the notoriety of the fact charged upon the Prisoner, and upon the whole matter they are resolved, and are agreed upon a Sentence to be pronounced against the Prisoner. But in respect he doth desire to be heard before the Sentence be read and pronounced, the Court hath resolved that they will hear him.

'Yet, Sir, this much I must tell you beforehand, which you have been minded of at other Courts, That if that which you have to say, be to offer any debate concerning the jurisdiction, you are not to be heard in it. You have offered it formerly, and you have struck at the root, that is, the Power and supreme authority of the Commons of England, which this Court will not admit a debate of, and which indeed it is an irrational thing in them to do, being a Court that acts upon authority derived from them. But, Sir, if you have anything to say in defence of yourself concerning the matter charged, the Court hath given me in command to let you know they will hear you.'

The King 'Since I see that you will not hear anything of debate concerning that which I confess I thought most material for the peace of the Kingdom, and for the liberty of the subject, I shall waive it, I shall speak nothing to it. But only I must tell you, that this many a day all things have been taken away from me, but that that I call dearer to me than my life, which is my conscience and my Honour. And if I had a respect to my life more than the Peace of the Kingdom, and the Liberty of the subject, certainly I should have made a particular defence for myself, for by that at least-wise I might have delayed an ugly sentence, which I believe will pass upon me. Therefore certainly Sir, as a man that hath some understanding, some knowledge of the World, if that my true Zeal to my Country had not overborn the care that I have for my own preservation, I should have gone another way to work than that I have done.

'Now, Sir, I conceive that an hasty Sentence once past may sooner be repented of, than recalled. And truly the self-same desire that I have for the peace of the Kingdom and the liberty of the subject, more than my own particular ends, makes me now at last desire, that I having something to say that concerns both, before Sentence be given, that I may be heard in the Painted Chamber before the Lords and Commons. This delay cannot be prejudicial unto you, whatsoever I say. If that I say be not reason, those that hear me must be judge, I cannot be judge of that that I have. If it be reason, and really for the welfare of the Kingdom, and the liberty of the subject, I am sure on it it is very well worth the hearing. Therefore I do conjure you, as you love that that you pretend, (I hope it is real) the liberty of the subject, the Peace of the Kingdom, that you will grant me this hearing before any Sentence be past. I only desire this, that you will take this into your consideration; it may be you have not heard of it beforehand. If you will, I will retire, and you may think of it, but if I cannot get this Liberty, I do protest, that these fair shows of liberty and peace are pure shows, and that you will not hear your King.'

The President 'Sir, you have now spoken.'

The King 'Yes, Sir.'

The President 'And this that you have said, is a further declining of the jurisdiction of this Court, which was the thing wherein you were limited before.'

The King 'Pray excuse me, Sir, for my interruption, because you mistake me. It is not a declining of it; you do judge me before you hear me speak. I say it will not, I do not decline it, though I cannot acknowledge the jurisdiction of the

Court. Yet, Sir, in this give me leave to say, I would do it, though I did not acknowledge it. In this I do protest, it is not the declining of it, since I say, if that I do say anything but that that is for the Peace of the Kingdom and liberty of the subject, then the shame is mine. Now I desire that you will take this into your consideration. If you will I will withdraw.'*

The President 'Sir, this is not altogether new that you have moved to us, not altogether new to us, though the first time in person you have offered it to the Court. Sir, you say you do not decline the jurisdiction of the Court.'

The King 'Not in this that I have said.'

The President 'I understand you well, Sir, but nevertheless that which you have offered, seems to be contrary to that saying of yours, for the Court are ready to give a Sentence. It is not, as you say, that they will not hear the King, for they have been ready to hear you, they have patiently waited your pleasure for three Courts together to hear what you would say to the people's Charge against you. To which you have not vouchsafed to give any answer at all. Sir, this tends to a further delay. Truly Sir, such delays as these, neither may the Kingdom nor justice well bear. You have had three several days to have offered in this kind what you would have pleased. This Court is founded upon that authority of the Commons of England, in whom rests the supreme jurisdiction. That which you now tender, is to have another jurisdiction, and a co-ordinate jurisdiction. I know very well you express yourself, Sir, that notwithstanding that you would offer to the Lords and Commons in the Painted Chamber, yet nevertheless you would proceed as here. I did hear you

---

*By this late stage Charles was anxious to speak but, even now, he would only do this provided his doing so was not interpreted as an acknowledgment of the Court's jurisdiction.

say so. But, Sir, that you would offer there, whatever it is, must needs be in delay of the justice here. So that if this Court be resolved and prepared for the Sentence, this that you offer, they are not bound to grant. But, Sir, according to that you seem to desire, and because you shall know the further pleasure of the Court upon that which you have moved, the Court will withdraw for a time.'*

This he did to prevent disturbance.

The King 'Shall I withdraw.'

The President 'Sir, you shall know the pleasure of the Court presently.'

The Court withdraws for half an hour into the Court of Wards.

The Serjeant at Arms 'The Court gives command that the Prisoner be withdrawn, until they give order for his return again.'

After which they returned, and being sat, the President commanded,

'Serjeant at Arms, send for your Prisoner,' who being come, the President proceeded.

The President 'Sir, you were pleased to make a motion here to the Court to offer a desire of yours touching the propounding of somewhat to the Lords and Commons in the Painted Chamber for the Peace of the Kingdom. Sir, you did in effect receive an answer before the Court adjourned. Truly Sir, their withdrawing and adjournment was *pro forma tantum*, for it did not seem to them that there was any difficulty in the thing. They have considered of what you have moved, and have considered of their own authority, which is founded, as it hath been often said, upon the supreme authority of the

---

*This adjournment may also have been due, as was later alleged, to the fact that John Downes, one of the judges, was about to rise and plead for clemency. For Downes's own account see Appendix.

Commons of England assembled in Parliament. The Court acts according to their commission. Sir, the return I have to you from the Court is this, that they have been too much delayed by you already, and this that you now offer, hath occasioned some little further delay, and they are judges appointed by the highest authority, and judges are no more to delay, than they are to deny justice. They are good words in the Great Old Charter of England, *Nulli Megabimus, nulli vendemus, nulli justisiam.** There must be no delay. But the truth is, Sir, and so every man here observes it, that you have much delayed them in your contempt and default, for which they might long since have proceeded to judgment against you, and notwithstanding what you have offered, they are resolved to proceed to Sentence and to judgment, and that is their unanimous consent.'

The King 'Sir, I know it is in vain for me to dispute, I am no sceptic for to deny the Power that you have, I know that you have power enough. Sir, I must confess I think it would have been for the Kingdom's peace, if you would have taken the pains to have shown the lawfulness of your power.

'For this delay that I have desired, I confess it is a delay, but it is a delay very important for the peace of the Kingdom. For it is not my person that I look at alone, it is the Kingdom's welfare and the Kingdom's peace.

'It is an old sentence, that we should think on long before we resolve on great matters suddenly . . . Therefore, Sir, I do say again, that I do put at your doors all the inconvenience of a hasty Sentence. I confess I have been here now I think this week, this day 8 days was the day I came here first. But a little delay of a day or two further may give peace, whereas

---

*Magna Carta, clause 40, reads: 'Nulli vendemus, nulli negabimus, aut differemus, rectum aut justiciam': To no one will we sell, to no one will we deny or delay right or justice.

a hasty judgment may bring on that trouble and perpetual inconvenience to the Kingdom that the child that is unborn may repent it. And therefore again, out of the duty I owe to God and to my Country, I do desire that I may be heard by the Lords and Commons in the Painted Chamber, or any other Chamber that you will appoint me.'

The President 'You have been already answered to what you even now moved, being the same you moved before, since the resolution and the judgment of the Court in it, and the Court now requires to know whether you have any more to say for yourself than you have said, before they proceed to Sentence.'

The King 'I say this, Sir, that if you hear me, if you will give me but this delay I doubt not but I shall give some satisfaction to you all here, and to my people after that, and therefore I do require you, as you will answer it at the dreadful day of judgment, that you will consider it once again.'

The President 'Sir, I have received direction from the Court.'

The King 'Well, Sir.'

The President 'If this must be reinforced, or anything of this nature, your answer must be the same, and they will proceed to Sentence, if you have nothing more to say.'

The King 'I have nothing more to say, but I shall desire that this may be entered what I have said.'

The President 'The Court then, Sir, hath something to say unto you, which I know, although I know it will be very unacceptable, yet notwithstanding they are willing and resolved to discharge their duty.'*

---

*Bradshaw followed with a long speech which is not given in Rushworth and which, since it consists mainly in a recapitulation of the arguments for the prosecution and is largely legal and historical, is not included here.

The King 'I would desire only one word before you give Sentence, and that is, that you would hear me concerning those great imputations that you have laid to my Charge.'

The President 'Sir, you must give me now leave to go on, for I am not far from your Sentence, and your time is now past.'

The King 'But I shall desire you will hear me a few words to you, for truly, whatever Sentence you will put upon me, in respect of those heavy imputations that I see by your speech you have put upon me. Sir, it is very true that—'

The President 'Sir, I must put you in mind. Truly, Sir, I would not willingly at this time especially interrupt you in anything you have to say that is proper for us to admit of. But, Sir, you have not owned us as a Court, and you look upon us as a sort of people met together, and we know what language we receive from your Party.'

The King 'I know nothing of that.'

The President 'You disavow us as a Court, and therefore for you to address yourself to us, and not to acknowledge us as a Court to judge of what you say, it is not to be permitted. And the truth is, all along from the first time you were pleased to disavow and disown us, the Court needed not to have heard you one word, for unless they be acknowledged a Court, and engaged, it is not proper for you to speak. Sir, we have given you too much liberty already, and admitted of too much delay, and we may not admit of any further, were it proper for us to do it, we should hear you freely, and we should not have declined to have heard you at large, what you could have said or proved on your behalf, whether for totally excusing, or for in part excusing those great and heinous charges that in whole or in part are laid upon you. But, Sir, I shall trouble you no longer, your sins are of so large a dimension, that if you do but seriously think of them, they will drive you to a sad consideration, and they may improve in you a sad and

serious repentance. And the Court doth heartily wish that
you may be so penitent for what you have done amiss, that
God may have mercy at leastwise on your better part. Truly,
Sir, for the other, it is our parts and duties to do that which
the Law prescribes. We are not here *jus dare*,* but *jus dicere*.†
We cannot be unmindful of what the Scripture tells us, for to
acquit the Guilty is of equal abomination as to condemn the
innocent. We may not acquit the guilty. What Sentence the
Law affirms to a Traitor, a Murderer, and a public Enemy
to the Country, that Sentence you are now to hear read unto
you, and that is the Sentence of the Court.

'Make an O Yes, and command silence while the Sentence
is read.'

   Which done, the Clerk read the Sentence drawn up in
Parchment.

Whereas the Commons of England assembled in Parliament
have by their late Act, entitled, *An Act of the Commons of England
assembled in Parliament for erecting an High Court of Justice for the
trying and judging of Charles Stuart, King of England*, authorised
and constituted us an High Court of Justice for the trying and
judging of the said Charles Stuart for the crimes and treasons
in the said Act mentioned. By virtue whereof the said Charles
Stuart hath been three several times convented before this
High Court, where the first day, being Saturday the 20th
January instant, in pursuance of the said Act, a Charge of
High Treason and other high crimes, was in the behalf of the
people of England, exhibited against him, and read openly
unto him, wherein he was and therein trusted with a limited
Power to govern by and according to the Law of the Land,

*To frame a law.
†To give judgment.

III

and not otherwise, and by his Trust, Oath, and Office, being obliged to use the Power committed to him, for the good and benefit of the People, and for the preservation of their rights and liberties, yet nevertheless out of a wicked design to erect and uphold in himself an unlimited and tyrannical Power to rule according to his Will, and to overthrow the Rights and Liberties of the People, and to take away and make void the foundations thereof, and of all redress and remedy of mis-government, which by the fundamental constitutions of this Kingdom were reserved on the Peoples behalf in the Right and Power of frequent and successive Parliaments, or national Meetings in Council, he, the said Charles Stuart, for accomplishment of such his designs, and for the protecting of himself and his adherents in his and their wicked practices, to the same end, hath traitorously and maliciously levyed War against the present Parliament, and People therein repre-sented, as with the circumstances of time and place is in the said Charge more particularly set forth, and that he hath thereby caused and procured many thousands of the free People of this Nation to be slain, and by Divisions, Parties, and Insurrections within this Land, by Invasions from foreign Parts, endeavoured and procured by him, and by many other evil ways and means, he, the said Charles Stuart, hath not only maintained and carried on the said War both by Sea and Land, but also hath renewed, or caused to be renewed, the said War against the Parliament, and good People of this Nation in this present year 1648 in several Counties and Places in this Kingdom in the Charge specified. And that he hath for that purpose given his Commission to his Son the Prince, and others, whereby, besides multitudes of other persons, many such as were by the Parliament entrusted and employed for the safety of this Nation, being by him or his Agents corrupted, to the betraying of their Trust, and

JOHN BRADSHAW
THE LORD PRESIDENT

revolting from the Parliament, have had entertainment and commission for the continuing and renewing of the War, and hostility against the said Parliament and People. And that by the said cruel and unnatural War so levyed, continued and renewed, much innocent blood of the free people of this Nation hath been spilt, many familes undone, the public Treasure wasted, trade obstructed, and miserably decayed, vast expense and damage to the Nation incurred, and many parts of the Land spoiled, some of them even to desolation. And that he still continues his commission to his said Son, and other Rebels and Revolters, both English and Foreigners, and to the Earl of Ormond, and to the Irish Rebels and Revolters associated with him, from whom further invasions of this Land, are threatened by his procurement, and on his behalf. And that all the said wicked designs, Wars, and evil practices of him the said Charles Stuart, were still carried on for the advancement and upholding of the personal interest of Will, Power, and pretended prerogative to himself and his family, against the public interest, common right, liberty, justice and peace of the people of this nation. And that he thereby hath been and is the occasioner, author, and continuer of the said unnatural, cruel and bloody Wars, and therein guilty of all the Treasons, Murders, Rapines, Burnings, Spoils, Desolations, Damage, and Mischief to this Nation, acted and committed in the said Wars, or occasioned thereby, whereupon the proceedings and judgment of this Court were prayed against him, as a Tyrant, Traitor, and Murderer, and public Enemy to the Commonwealth, as by the said Charge more fully appeareth. To which Charge, being read unto him as aforesaid, he, the said Charles Stuart, was required to give his answer, but he refused so to do, and upon Monday the 22nd day of January, instant, being again brought before this Court, and there required to answer directly to the said Charge, he still refused so to do. Whereupon his default and contumacy was entered, and the next day, being the third time brought before the Court, Judgment was then prayed against him on the behalf of the People of England for his contumacy, and for the matters contained against him in the said Charge, as taking the same for confest, in regard of his refusing to answer thereto. Yet notwithstanding this Court (not willing to take advantage of his contempt) did once more require him to answer to the said Charge, but he again refused to do so. Upon which his several defaults, this Court might justly have proceeded to Judgment against him both for his contumacy, and the matters of the Charge, taking the same for confest as aforesaid.

Yet nevertheless the Court, for its own clearer information, and further satisfaction, have thought fit to examine Witnesses upon Oath, and take notice of other evidences, touching the matters contained in the said Charge, which accordingly they have done.

Now therefore upon serious and mature deliberation of the Premises, and consideration had of the notoriety of the matters of fact charged upon him as aforesaid, this Court is in Judgment and conscience satisfied that he, the said Charles Stuart, is guilty of levying War against the said Parliament and people, and maintaining and continuing the same, for which in the said Charge he stands accused. And by the general course of his Government, Counsels and Practices, before and since this Parliament began (which have been and are notorious and public, and the effects whereof remain abundantly upon record) this Court is fully satisfied in their Judgments and Consciences, that he has been and is guilty of the wicked designs and endeavours in the said Charge set forth, and that the said War hath been levyed, maintained and continued by him as aforesaid, in prosecution, and for accomplishment of the said designs and that he hath been and is the occasioner, author, and continuer of the said unnatural, cruel, and bloody wars, and therein guilty of High Treason, and of the Murders, Rapines, Burnings, Spoils, Desolations, Damage and Mischief to this Nation acted and committed in the said War, and occasioned thereby. For all which Treasons and Crimes this Court doth adjudge, that he, the said Charles Stuart, as a Tyrant, Traitor, Murderer, and public Enemy to the good people of this Nation shall be put to Death by severing of his Head from his Body.*

Which being read the President added:

The President 'The Sentence now read, and published, is the Act, Sentence, Judgment and Resolution of the whole Court.'

To which they all expressed their assent by standing up, as was before agreed and ordered.

His Majesty then said:

The King 'Will you hear me a word, Sir?'

The President 'Sir, you are not to be heard after the Sentence.'

The King 'No, Sir?'

The President 'No, Sir, by your favour, Sir. Guard, withdraw your Prisoner.'

The King 'I may speak after Sentence. By your favour, Sir, I may speak after Sentence, ever. By your favour—hold. The Sentence, Sir,—I say, Sir, I do—I am not suffered for to speak. Expect what justice other people will have.'

His Majesty being taken away by the Guard, as he passed down the Stairs, the Soldiers scoffed at him, casting the

---

*The death warrant (now in the library of the House of Lords) was signed by fifty-nine of the judges.

smoke of their tobacco (a thing very distasteful unto him) and throwing their pipes in his way.

As he passed along, hearing the rabble of soldiers crying out, Justice, Justice, he said, 'Poor Soldiers, for a piece of money they would do so for their commanders.'

PART III

PART III

THE LAST HOURS

Sir Thomas Herbert's Account

THE King, at the rising of the Court, was with a guard of Halberdiers returned to Whitehall in a close chair,* through King Street, both sides whereof had a guard of Foot-soldiers, who were silent as his Majesty passed. But shop stalls and windows were full of people, many of which shed tears, and some of them with audible voices prayed for the King, who through the privy-garden was carried to his bed-chamber; whence, after two hours space, he was removed to St James's. Nothing of the fear of death, or indignities offered, seemed a terror, or provoked him to impatience, nor uttered he a reproachful word reflecting upon any of his judges (albeit he well knew that some of them had been his domestic servants) or against any Member of the House, or officer of the Army; so wonderful was his patience, though his spirit was great, and might otherwise have expressed his resent-ments upon several occasions. It was a true Christian-fortitude to have the mastery of his passion, and submission to the will of God under such temptations.

The King now bidding farewell to the world, his whole business was a serious preparation for death, which opens the door unto Eternity; in order thereunto, he laid aside all other thoughts, and spent the remainder of his time in prayer and other pious exercises of devotion, and in conference with that meek and learned Bishop Dr Juxon,† who under God, was a

*A sedan chair.
†Bishop of London.

great support to him in that his afflicted condition: and
resolving to sequester himself, so as he might have no disturbance to his mind, nor interruption to his meditations; he
ordered Mr Herbert to excuse it to any that might have the
desire to visit him. I know (said the King) my nephew, the
Prince-Elector,* will endeavour it, and some other lords that
love me, which I would take in good part, but my time is
short and precious, and I am desirous to improve it the best I
may in preparation; I hope they will not take it ill, that none
have access unto me but my children. The best office they
can do now, is to pray for me. And it fell out accordingly:
for his Electoral Highness, accompanied by the Duke of
Richmond, the Lord Marquis of Hertford, the Earls of Southampton, and Lindsey, with some more, having got leave,
came to the bedchamber door, where Mr Herbert, pursuant
to the King's command, acquainted the Prince-Elector, and
those noblemen, with what the King gave him in charge;
wherein they acquiesced, and presenting their humble duty
to his Majesty, with their prayers, they returned with hearts
full of sorrow, as appeared by their faces. The Prince also†
(then in Holland) by the States Ambassadors interceded with
the Parliament, and used all possible means with the Army to
prevent, or at least for deferring of execution.

At this time also came to St James's Mr Calmy, Mr Vines,
Mr Caryll, Mr Dell, and some other London Ministers, who
presented their duty to the King, with their humble desires
to pray with him, and perform other offices of service, if his
Majesty pleased to accept of them. The King returned them
thanks for their love to his soul, hoping that they, and all

*Charles Louis, Elector Palatine, eldest son of Charles's sister Eliza-
beth (the Winter Queen) and Frederick, Elector of the Palatinate, and
brother to Prince Rupert.
†Prince of Wales, future Charles II.

other his good subjects, would, in their addresses to God, be mindful of him. But in regard he had made choice of Dr Juxon (whom for many years he had known to be a pious and learned divine, and able to administer ghostly comfort to his soul, suitable to his present condition) he would have none other. These Ministers were no sooner gone, but Mr John Goodwyn (Minister in Coleman Street) came likewise upon the same account, to tender his Service, which the King also thanked him for, and dismissed him with the like friendly answer.

Mr Herbert about this time going to the cockpit near Whitehall, where the Earl of Pembroke's lodgings were, he then, as at sundry other times, enquired how his Majesty did, and gave his humble duty to him, and withal, asked him if his Majesty had the gold watch he sent for, and how he liked it. Mr Herbert assured his Lordship, the King had not yet received it. The Earl fell presently into a passion, marvelling thereat; being the more troubled, lest his Majesty should think him careless, in observing his commands; and told Mr Herbert, at the King's coming to St James's, as he was sitting under the great Elm Tree, near Sir Benjamin Ruddier's Lodge in the Park, seeing a considerable military officer of the Army pass towards St James's, he went to meet him, and demanding of him, if he knew his Cousin Tom Herbert, that waited on the King, the officer said, he did, and was going to St James's. The Earl then delivered to him the gold watch that had the alarm, desiring him to give it Mr Herbert, to present it to the King. The officer promised the Earl he would immediately do it. My Lord (said Mr Herbert) I have sundry times seen and passed by that Officer since, and do assure your Lordship he had not delivered it me according to your order and promise, nor said anything to me concerning it, nor has the King it I am certain. The Earl was very angry; and gave the officer his due character, and threatened to question him. But such was the severity of the times, that it was then judged dangerous to reflect upon such a person, being a favourite of the time, so as no notice was taken of it. Nevertheless, Mr Herbert (at the Earl's desire) acquainted his Majesty therewith, who gave the Earl his thanks, and said: 'Ah! Had he not told the officer it was for me, it would probably have been delivered; he well knew how short a time I could enjoy it.' This relation is in prosecution of what is formerly mentioned, concerning the clock or alarm watch his Majesty intended to dispose of, as is declared.

That evening, Mr Seymour (a gentleman then attending the Prince of Wales in his bedchamber) by Colonel Hacker's permission, came to his Majesty's bedchamber door, desiring to speak with the King from the Prince of Wales; being admitted, he presented his Majesty with a letter from his Highness the Prince of Wales, bearing date from the Hague the 23rd day of January 1648 (Old Style). Mr Seymour, at his entrance, fell into a passion, having formerly seen his Majesty in a glorious state, and now in a dolorous; and having kissed the King's hand, clasped about his legs, lamentably mourning. Hacker came in with the gentlemen and was abashed. But so soon as his Majesty had read his son's sorrowing letter, and heard what his servant had to say, and imparted to him what his Majesty thought fit in return, the Prince's servant took his leave, and was no sooner gone, but the King went to his devotion, Dr Juxon praying with him, and reading some select chapters out of sacred Scripture.

That evening the King took a ring from his finger, and gave it Mr Herbert; it had an emerald set between two diamonds, and commanded him as late as it was to go with it from St James's to a Lady* living then in Channel Row, on the backside of King Street, in Westminster, and give it to

*She was the King's laundress, and wife to Sir W. Wheeler. *Author's note.*

her, without saying anything. The night was exceeding dark and guards set in several places, as the house, garden, park, gates near Whitehall, King Street, and other where.

Nevertheless, getting the word from Colonel Thomlinson, (then there, and in all places wherever he was about the King so civil both towards his Majesty and such as attended him, as gained him the King's good opinion; and as an evidence thereof, gave him his gold pick-tooth case, as he was one time walking in the presence-chamber) Mr Herbert passed currently, though in all places where sentinels were, he was bid stand, till the corporals had the word from him. Being arrived at the Lady's house, he delivered her the ring. 'Sir' (said she) 'give me leave to show you the way into the parlour,' where she desired him to stay till she returned, which in a little time she did, and gave him a little cabinet which was closed with three seals; two of them being the King's Arms, the third was the figure of a Roman; praying him to deliver it the same hand that sent the ring, which was left her.

The word secured Mr Herbert's return unto the King. When the Bishop being but newly gone to his lodging in Sir Henry Hen's house near St James's Gate, his Majesty said to Mr Herbert, he should see it opened in the morning.

Morning being come, the Bishop was early with the King and after prayers his Majesty broke the seals open, and showed them what was contained in it; there were diamonds and jewels, most part broken Georges and Garters.* You see (said he) all the wealth now in my power to give my two children.

Next day Princess Elizabeth, and the Duke of Gloucester,†

*The insignia of the Order of the Garter.
†Elizabeth, Charles's second daughter, was just 14. Overwhelmed with grief at her father's death she died at Carisbrook the following year. Henry, Duke of Gloucester, was Charles's third son, aged 9. He was allowed to leave the country in 1652, returned to England with Charles II in 1660 and died that year of smallpox.

her brother, came to take their sad farewell of the King their father, and to ask his blessing. This was the 29th January. The Princess being the elder, was the most sensible of her Royal Father's condition, as appeared by her sorrowful look and excessive weeping; and her little brother seeing his sister weep, he took the like impression, though by reason of his tender age he could not have the like apprehension. The King raised them both from off their knees; he kissed them, gave them his blessing, and setting them on his knees, admonished them concerning their duty and loyal observance to the Queen their mother, the Prince that was his successor, love to the Duke of York,* and his other relations. The King then gave them all his jewels, save the George he wore, which was cut in an Onyx with great curiosity, and set about with 21 fair diamonds, and the reverse set with the like number; and again kissing his children, had such pretty and pertinent answers from them both, as drew tears of joy and love from his eyes; and then praying God Almighty to bless 'em, he turned about, expressing a tender and fatherly affection. Most sorrowful was this parting, the young Princess shedding tears and crying lamentably, so as moved others to pity, that formerly were hard-hearted; and at opening the bedchamber door, the King returned hastily from the window and kissed 'em and blessed 'em; so parted.

This demonstration of a pious affection exceedingly comforted the King in this his affliction; so that in a grateful return he went immediately to prayer, the good Bishop and Mr Herbert being only present.

It may not be forgotten, that Sir Henry Herbert, Knight Master of the Revels, and Gentleman in Ordinary of his Majesty's Honourable Privy-Chamber (one that cordially loved and honoured the King his Master, and during the

*Charles's second son, later James II.

War, suffered considerably in his estate by sequestration and otherwise) meeting Mr Herbert his kinsman in St James's Park, first enquired how his Majesty did? He then presented his humble duty to the King, with an assurance that himself and many others of his Majesty's servants fervently prayed for him, and requested that his Majesty would please to read the second chapter of Ecclesiasticus; for he would find comfort in it, aptly suiting his present condition. Accordingly Mr Herbert soon after acquainted the King therewith, who thanked Sir Henry, and commended him for his excellent parts, being a good scholar, soldier, and an accomplished courtier; and for his many years faithful service much valued by the King, who presently turned to the chapter, and read it with much satisfaction.

That day the Bishop of London, after prayers, preached before the King; his text was the second chapter of the Romans, and sixteenth verse. The words are, 'At that day when God shall judge the secrets of men by Jesus Christ,' etc., inferring from thence, that although God's Judgments be for some time deferred, he will nevertheless proceed to a strict Examination of what is both said and done by every man; yea, the most hidden things and imaginations of men will most certainly be made to appear at the Day of Judgment, when the Lord Jesus Christ shall be upon his high Tribunal; all Designs, tho concealed in this Life, shall then be plainly discovered; he then proceeded to the present sad occasion, and after that, administered the Sacrament. That day the King eat and drank very sparingly, most part of the day being spent in prayer and meditation; it was some hours after Night, e'er Dr Juxon took leave of the King, who willed him to be early with him the next morning.

That night, after which sentence was pronounced in Westminster Hall, Colonel Hacker (who then commanded the guards about the King) would have placed two Musqueteers in the King's bedchamber, which his Majesty being acquainted with, he made no reply, only gave a sigh; howbeit the good Bishop and Mr Herbert, apprehending the horror of it, and disturbance it would give the King in his meditations and preparation for his departure out of this uncomfortable world; also representing the barbarousness of such an act, they never left the Colonel till he reversed his order by withdrawing these men.

After the Bishop was gone to his lodging, the King continued reading and praying more than two hours after. The King commanded Mr Herbert to lie by his bedside upon a pallat, where he took small rest, that being the last night his Gracious Sovereign and Master enjoyed; but nevertheless the King for four hours or thereabouts, slept soundly, and awaking about two hours afore day, he opened his curtain to call Mr Herbert; there being a great cake of wax set in a silver bason, that then as at all other times, burned all night; so that he perceived him somewhat disturbed in sleep; but calling him bad him rise; for (said his Majesty) I will get up, having a great work to do this day; however he would know why he was so troubled in his sleep? He replied, 'May it please your Majesty I was dreaming.' 'I would know your Dream,' said the King; which being told,* his Majesty said, 'It was remarkable. Herbert, this is my second Marriage Day; I would be as trim to day as may be; for before night I hope to be espoused to my blessed Jesus.' He then appointed what clothes he would wear; 'Let me have a shirt on more than ordinary,' said the King, 'by reason the season is so sharp as probably may make me shake, which some observers will imagine proceeds from fear. I would have no such imputation. I fear not death! Death is not terrible to me. I bless my God I am prepared.'

*For Herbert's later and fuller account of this dream, see Appendix D.

These, or words to this effect, his Majesty spoke to Mr Herbert, as he was making ready. Soon after came Dr Juxon, Bishop of London, precisely at the time his Majesty the night before had appointed him. Mr Herbert then falling upon his knees, humbly begged his Majesty's pardon, if he had at any time been negligent in his duty, whilst he had the honour to serve him. The King thereupon gave him his hand to kiss, having the day before been graciously pleased, under his royal hand, to give him a certificate, expressing, that the said Mr Herbert, was not imposed upon him, but by his Majesty made choice of to attend him in his bedchamber, and had served him with faithfulness and loyal affection. At the same time his Majesty also delivered him his Bible, in the margin whereof he had with his own hand writ many annotations and quotations, and charged him to give it the Prince so soon as he returned; repeating what he had enjoined the Princess Elizabeth, his daughter, That he would be dutiful and indulgent to the Queen his Mother (to whom his Majesty writ two days before by Mr Seymour), affectionate to his brothers and sisters, who also were to be observant and dutiful to him their sovereign; and for as much as from his heart he had forgiven his enemies, and in perfect charity with all men would leave the world, he had advised the Prince his son to exceed in mercy, not in rigour; and, as to episcopacy, it was still his opinion, that it is of apostolique institution, and in this kingdom exercised from the primitive times, and therein, as in all other his affairs, prayed God to vouchsafe him, both in reference to Church and State, a pious and discerning spirit; and that it was his last and earnest request, that he would frequently read the Bible, which in all the time of his affliction had been his best instructor and delight; and to meditate upon what he read; as also such other books as might improve his knowledge. He likewise commanded Mr Herbert to give

his son, the Duke of York, his large ring sun-dial of silver, a
jewel his Majesty much valued; it was invented and made by
Mr Delamaine, an able mathematician, who projected it,
and in a little printed book showed its excellent use, in
resolving many questions in arithmetic, and other rare opera-
tions to be wrought by it in the mathematics. To the Princess
Elizabeth *Doctor Andrew's Sermons* (he was Prelate of the most
noble Order of the Garter, as he was Bishop of Winchester),
Archbishop Laud against Fisher the Jesuit, which book (the King
said) would ground her against Popery, and Mr Hooker's
Ecclesiastical Polity. To the Duke of Gloucester, *King James's
Works*, and Dr Hammond's *Practical Catechism*. *Cassandra** to
the Earl of Lindsey, the Lord High Chamberlain. And his
gold watch to the Duchess of Richmond. All which, as
opportunity served, Mr Herbert delivered.

His Majesty then bade him withdraw; for he was about an
hour in private with the Bishop; and being called in, the
Bishop went to prayer; and reading also the 27th chapter of
the Gospel of St Matthew, which relateth the Passion of our
Blessed Saviour. The King, after the Service was done, asked
the Bishop, if he had made choice of that Chapter, being so
applicable to his present condition? The Bishop replied,
'May it please your Gracious Majesty, it is the proper lesson
for the day, as appears by the Calendar;' which the King was
much affected with, so aptly serving as a seasonable preparation for his death that day.

So as his Majesty, abandoning all thoughts of earthly concerns, continued in prayer and meditation, and concluded
with a cheerful submission to the will and pleasure of the

---

*A romance by Gautier de la Calprenède (c. 1610–63), dealing with
more or less imaginary events in the life of Alexander the Great. It was
a fashionable work but not translated until about 1652, so the copy given
to Lindsey must have been the French original.

Almighty, saying, He was ready to resign himself into the hands of Christ Jesus, being with the Kingly Prophet, shut up in the hands of his enemies; as is expressed in the 31st Psalm, and the 8th Verse.

Colonel Hacker then knocked easily at the King's chamber door. Mr Herbert being within, would not stir to ask who it was; but knocking the second time a little louder, the King bade him go to the door. He guessed his business. So Mr Herbert demanding, Wherefore he knocked? The Colonel said, he would speak with the King. The King said, 'Let him come in.' The Colonel in trembling manner came near, and told his Majesty, it was time to go to Whitehall, where he might have some further time to rest. The King bad him go forth, he would come presently. Some time his Majesty was private, and afterwards taking the good Bishop by the hand, looking upon him with a cheerful countenance, he said, 'Come, let us go;' and bidding Mr Herbert take with him the silver clock, that hung by the bed side, said, 'Open the door, Hacker has given us a second warning.' Through the garden the King passed into the Park, where making a stand, he asked Mr Herbert the hour of the day; and taking the clock into his hand, gave it him, and bade him keep it in memory of him; which Mr Herbert keeps accordingly.

The Park had several Companies of Foot drawn up, who made a Guard on either side as the King passed, and a Guard of Halberdiers in company went some before, and othersome followed; and drums beat, and the noise was so great as one could hardly hear what another spoke.

Upon the King's right hand went the Bishop, and Colonel Thomlinson on his left, with whom his Majesty had some discourse by the way; Mr Herbert was next the King; after him the Guards. In this manner went the King through the Park; and coming to the stair, the King passed along the galleries unto his bedchamber, where, after a little repose, the Bishop went to prayer; which, being done, his Majesty bid Mr Herbert bring him some bread and wine, which being brought, the King broke the manchet,* and eat a mouthful of it, and drank a small glassful of the claret-wine, and then was sometime in private with the Bishop, expecting when Hacker would the third and last time give warning. Mean time his Majesty told Mr Herbert which satin nightcap he would use, which being provided, and the King at private prayer, Mr Herbert addressed himself to the Bishop, and told him, the King had ordered him to have a white satin nightcap ready, but was not able to endure the sight of that violence they upon the scaffold would offer the King. The good Bishop bid him then give him the Cap, and wait at the end of the Banquetting House, near the scaffold, to take care of the King's body; for (said he) that, and his interment, will be our last office.

Colonel Hacker came soon after to the bedchamber door, and gave his last signal; the Bishop and Mr Herbert, weeping, fell upon their knees, and the King gave them his hand to kiss, and helped the Bishop up, for he was aged.

Colonel Hacker attending still at the chamber door, the King took notice of it, and said, 'Open the door,' and bade Hacker go, he would follow. A guard was made all along the galleries and the Banquetting House; but behind the soldiers abundance of men and women crowded in, though with some peril to their persons, to behold the saddest sight England ever saw. And as his Majesty passed by, with a cheerful look, heard them pray for him, the soldiers not rebuking any of them; by their silence and dejected faces seeming afflicted rather than insulting. There was a passage broken through the wall, by which the King passed unto the scaffold.

*A small loaf or roll of fine wheaten bread.

PART IV

THE EXECUTION

John Rushworth's Account

THE scaffold was hung round with black, and the floor covered with black, and the axe and block laid in the middle of the scaffold. There were divers companies of Foot and Horse on every side the scaffold, and the multitudes of people that came to be spectators were very great. The King making a pass upon the scaffold, looked very earnestly on the block, and asked Colonel Hacker if there were no higher, and then spoke thus, directing his speech to the gentlemen on the scaffold.

King 'I shall be very little heard of any body here, I shall therefore speak a word unto you here. Indeed I could hold my peace very well, if I did not think that holding my peace would make some men think that I did submit to the guilt, as well as to the punishment. But I think it is my duty to God first, and to my Country, for to clear myself both as an honest man, a good king, and a good christian. I shall begin first with my innocence. In troth, I think it not very needful for me to insist long upon this, for all the world knows I never did begin the war with the two Houses of Parliament, and I call God to witness (to whom I must shortly make an account) that I never did intend to incroach upon their privileges. They began upon me. It is the militia they began upon, they confest that the Militia was mine, but they thought it fit to have it from me. And to be short, if anybody will look but to the dates of the commissions, their commissions and mine, and likewise to the declarations, will see clearly that they began these unhappy troubles, not I. So that as to the guilt of these enormous Crimes that are laid against me, I hope in God, that God will clear me of it, I will not, I'm in Charity. God forbid that I should lay it upon the two Houses of Parliament, there is no necessity of either. I hope they are free of this guilt for I believe that ill instruments between them and me, has been the chief cause of all this bloodshed, so that by way of speaking, as I find myself clear of this, I hope (and pray God) that they may too. Yet for all this God forbid that I should be so ill a christian, as not to say that God's Judgments are just upon me, many times he does pay justice by an unjust Sentence, that is ordinary. I only say this, that an unjust Sentence (*meaning Strafford*) that I suffered to take effect, is punished now by an unjust Sentence upon me, that is, so far I have said to show you that I am an innocent man. Now for to show you that I am a good Christian. I hope there is (*pointing to Dr Juxon*) a good man that will bear me witness. That I have forgiven all the world, and even those in particular that have been the chief causers of my death, who they are God knows, I do not desire to know, I pray God forgive them. But this is not all. My charity must go further; I wish that they may repent, for indeed they have committed a great sin in that particular. I pray God with St Stephen, that this be not laid to their Charge; nay not only so, but that they may take the right way to the peace of the Kingdom, for charity commands me not only to forgive particular men, but my charity commands me to endeavour to the last gasp the peace of the Kingdom. So, Sirs, I do wish with all my soul, and I do hope there is some here will carry it further, that they may endeavour the peace of the Kingdom. Now, Sirs, I must show you both how you are out of the way, and I will put you in the way. First you are out of the way, for certainly all the way you ever have had yet, as I could find by anything, is in the way of conquest. Certainly this is an ill way, for conquest, Sirs, in my opinion is never just, except there be a good just cause, either for matter of wrong, or just Title, and then if you go beyond it, the first quarrel that you have to it, that makes it unjust at the end, that was just at first. But if it be only matter of conquest, then it is a great robbery. As a Pirate said to Alexander the Great, that he was the great robber, he was but a petty robber, and so, Sirs, I do think the way that you are in, is much out of the way. Now Sirs, for to put you in the way, believe it, you will never do right, nor God will never prosper you, until you give him his due, the King his due (that is, my successors) and the people their due, I am as much for them as any of you. You must give God his due, by regulating rightly his Church (according to his Scriptures) which is now out of order, for to set you in a way particularly, now I cannot, but only this. A National Synod freely called, freely debating among themselves, must settle this, when that every opinion is freely and clearly heard. For the King indeed I will not. *Then turning to a gentleman that touched the Axe, he said "Hurt not the axe that may hurt me".* As for the King, the Laws of the Land will clearly instruct you for that, therefore because it concerns my own particular, I only give you a touch of it. For the People, and truly I desire their liberty and freedom, as much as anybody whomsoever, but I must tell you, that their liberty and freedom consist in having of Government, those laws by which their life and their goods may be most their own. It is not for having share in Government, Sirs; that is nothing pertaining to them. A subject and a sovereign are clean different things, and therefore, until they do that, I mean, that you do put the people in that liberty as I say, certainly they will never enjoy themselves. Sirs, it was for this that now I am come here. If I would have given way to an arbitrary way, for to have all laws changed according to the Power of the Sword, I needed not to have come here, and therefore I tell you, (and I pray God it be not laid to your Charge), that I am the Martyr of the people. In troth, Sirs, I shall not hold you much longer, for I will only say this to you, that in truth I could have desired some little time longer, because that I would have put this that I have said in a little more order, and a little better digested, than I have done, and therefore, I hope you will excuse me. I have delivered my conscience, I pray God that you take those courses that are best for the good of the Kingdom, and your own salvation.'

Dr Juxon 'Will your Majesty, though it may be very well known your Majesty's affections to religion, yet it may be expected that you should say somewhat for the World's satisfaction in that particular.'

The King 'I thank you very heartily my Lord, for that I had almost forgotten it. In troth Sirs, my conscience in Religion, I think is very well known to the world, and therefore I declare before you all, that I die a christian according to the profession of the Church of England as I found it left me by my Father, and this honest man (*meaning the Bishop*) I think will witness it.' Then turning to the Officers, said: 'Sirs, excuse me for this same, I have a good cause, and I have a gracious God. I will say no more.' Then turning to Colonel Hacker he said, 'Take care that they do not put me to pain, and Sir, this and it please you—' But then a gentleman coming near the axe, the King said, 'Take heed of the Axe, pray take heed of the Axe.' Then the King speaking to the Executioner, said, 'I shall say but very short prayers, and then thrust out my hands.' Then the King called to Dr Juxon for his nightcap, and having put it on, he said to the Executioner, 'Does my hair trouble you.' Who desired him to put it all under his cap,

which the King did accordingly by the help of the Executioner and the Bishop. Then the King turning to Dr Juxon,
said, 'I have a good cause and a gracious God on my side.'

Dr Juxon 'There is but one stage more. This stage is turbu-
lent and troublesome, it is a short one. But you may consider
it will soon carry you a very great way, it will carry you from
earth to heaven, and there you shall find to your great joy
the prize. You haste to a crown of glory.'

The King 'I go from a corruptible to an incorruptible
Crown, where no disturbance can be.'

Dr Juxon 'You are exchanged from a temporal to an eternal
Crown, a good exchange.'

Then the King took off his cloak and his George, giving his
George to Dr Juxon, saying, 'Remember,' (it is thought for
the Prince) and some other small ceremonies [were] past.
After which the King stooping down, laid his neck upon the
block. And after a little pause, stretching forth his hands, the
Executioner at one blow severed his head from his body.

PART V

THE FUNERAL

Sir Thomas Herbert's Account

MR Herbert, during this, was at the door lamenting; and the Bishop coming thence with the Royal Corpse, which was immediately coffined, and covered with a black velvet-pall; he and Mr Herbert went with it to the back stairs to be embalmed. Mean time they went into the Long-Gallery, where chancing to meet the General,* he asked Mr Herbert, how the King did? Which he thought strange: it seems thereby that the General knew not what had passed, being all that morning (as indeed at other times) using his Power and interest to have the execution deferred for some days, forbearing his coming among the officers, and fully resolved, with his own regiment, to prevent the execution, or have it deferred till he could make a party in the Army to second his design; but being with the officers of the Army then at prayer, or discourse in Colonel Harrison's appartment (being a room at the hither end of that gallery looking towards the Privy Garden) his question being answered, the General seemed much surprised; and walking further in the gallery, they were met by another great Commander, Cromwell, who knew what had so lately passed; for he told them, they should have orders for the King's Burial speedily.

The Royal Corpse being embalmed and coffined, and those wrapped in lead, and covered with a new velvet-pall,

*Fairfax, though this story seems most unlikely, and may be due to a lapse of memory on Herbert's part.

was removed to the King's house at St James's, where was great pressing by all sorts of people to see the King, or where he was: A doleful spectacle! but few had leave to enter and behold it.

Where to bury the King was the last duty remaining. By some historians it's said, that the King spoke something to the Bishop concerning his Burial.

Mr Herbert, both before and after the King's death, was frequently in company with the Bishop, and affirms, that the Bishop never mentioned anything to him of the King's naming any place where he would be buried; nor did Mr Herbert (who constantly attended his Majesty) hear him at any time declare his mind concerning it; nor was it in his life time a proper question for either of them to ask, albeit they had often times the opportunity, especially when his Majesty was bequeathing to his royal children and friends what is formerly related. Nor did the Bishop declare anything concerning the place to Mr Herbert, which doubtless he would, upon Mr Herbert's pious care about it, which being duly considered, they thought no place more fit to inter the corpse, than in King Henry VII's Chapel, at the East end of Westminster Abbey, out of which King's loins King Charles was lineally extracted, and where several Kings and Queens descending from King Henry VII are interred, namely, King Edward VI, Queen Mary, Queen Elizabeth, Mary, Queen of Scots, King James, Prince Henry, and other Princes of the Royal Stem.

Whereupon, Mr Herbert made his application to such as were then in power, for leave to bury the King's body in King Henry VII's Chapel, among his ancestors; but his request was denied, this reason being given, that probably it would attract infinite numbers of people of all sorts thither, to see where the King was buried, which (as the times then were) was judged unsafe and inconvenient. Mr Herbert acquainting the Bishop therewith, they then resolved to bury the King's body in the Royal Chapel of St George within the Castle of Windsor, both in regard his Majesty was Sovereign of the most noble Order of the Garter; and that several Kings, his ancestors are there interred, namely, King Henry VI, King Edward IV, and King Henry VIII. It was also a Castle and place his Majesty took great delight in, as in discourse he oft times expressed as occasion offered; and withal, for that the Royal Chapel of St George was, though founded by King Edward III, rebuilt by King Edward IV with much more magnificence.

Upon which considerations Mr Herbert made his second address to the committee of Parliament, who, after some deliberation, gave him an order bearing date the 6th of February 1649 authorizing him and Mr Mildmay to bury the King's body there, which the Governor was to observe.

Accordingly the corpse was thither carried from St James's in a hearse covered with black velvet, drawn by six horses also covered with black; after which four coaches followed, two of them covered likewise with black cloth, in which were about a dozen gentlemen and others, most of them being such as had waited on his Majesty at Carisbrook Castle and other places, since his Majesty's going from Newcastle, all of them being in black.

Being come to Windsor Castle, Mr Herbert showed the Governor, Colonel Whitchcott, the Committee's Order for permitting Mr Herbert and Mr Mildmay to bury the late King in any place within Windsor Castle they should think meet.

In the first place in order thereto, they carried the King's body into the Dean's House, which all was hung with black by Richard Harrison, and then to his usual bedchamber, which is within the Palace; after which they went into St George's Chapel, to take a view thereof, and of the most fit and honourable place for the Royal Corpse to rest in. Having taken a view, they at first thought, that the Tomb House would be a fit place; it was erected by the magnificent Prelate Cardinal Wolsey (much about the same time he built his stately House at Hampton Court, in which Tomb House he begun a glorious monument for his great master King Henry VIII), but this place, though adjoining, yet not being within the Royal Chapel, they waived it. For if King Henry VIII were buried there (albeit to that day the place of his burial was unknown to any) yet in regard his Majesty (who was a real Defender of the Faith, and as far from censuring any as might be) would upon occasional discourse express some dislike of King Harry's proceedings, in misemploying those vast revenues the suppressed Abbeys, Monasteries, and other religious houses were endowed with, and by demolishing those many stately structures (which both expressed the greatness of the founders, and preserved the splendour of the kingdom) might at the Reformation have in some measure been kept up and converted to sundry pious uses. Upon consideration thereof, these gentlemen declined it, and pitched upon the vault where King Edward IV is interred being in the North side of the Choir, near the Altar as formerly remembered, that King being one his late Majesty would many times make mention of, and from whom his Majesty was lineally propagated, which induced Mr Herbert to give order to have that vault opened, to bury the King's body near his ancestor King Edward IV who is interred under a fair large stone of Tuke, raised within the opposite arch, having a range of iron bars gilt, curiously cut according to church work; there is no sculpture or inscription, only the royal badge painted on the inside of the arch in several places.

But as they were about his work, some noblemen came thither, namely, the Duke of Richmond, the Marquis of Hertford, since Duke of Somerset, the Earl of Southampton, the Earl of Lindsey, Lord High-Chamberlain, with Dr Juxon, Lord Bishop of London (Archbishop of Canterbury afterwards) who had leave to attend the King's body to his grave; and being fit to submit and leave the choice of the place of burial to those great persons, they in like manner, viewing the Tomb House, and the Choir, one of those Lords beating gently upon the pavement with his staff, perceived a hollow sound, and ordering the stones and earth thereunder to be removed, discovered a descent into a vault, where two coffins were laid near one another, the one very large of antique form, the other little, supposed to contain the bodies of King Henry VIII and Queen Jane Seymour, his third wife, and mother of King Edward VI of whom in the year 1537 she died in childbed; and may be credited; for as Mr Brook, York Herald, in his catalogue of the nobility, p. 40 observes, no other of King Harry's six wives was buried at Windsor; the velvet-palls that were over them seem fresh, albeit laid there 130 years and upwards. The Lords agreeing that the King's body should there be interred (being about the middle of the Choir, over against the eleventh stall upon the sovereigns side) they gave order to have the King's name, and year he died, cut in lead, which whilst the workman was about, the Lords went out, and gave the Sexton order to lock the Chapel door, not suffering any to stay till further notice. The Sexton did his best to clear the Chapel; nevertheless (he said) a foot soldier had hid himself so as was not discerned, and being greedy of prey, got into the vault, and cut so much of the velvet-pall, as he judged would hardly be missed, and wimbled a hole* into the coffin that was largest, probably

*Made a hole with a gimlet.

fancying there was something well worth his adventure. The Sexton, at his opening the door, espied the sacrilegious person, who being searched, a bone was also found about him, which, he said, he would haft a knife with. The Governor gave him his reward. But this manifests that a real body was there, which some that have hard thoughts of King Harry, have scrupled.

The Girdle or Circumscription of Capital Letters in Lead put about the coffin, had only these words,

KING CHARLES,

1648*

The King's body was then brought from his bedchamber down into St George's Hall, whence, after a little stay, it was with a slow and solemn pace (much sorrow in most faces discernable) carried by gentlemen that were of some quality, and in mourning. The Lords in like habits followed the royal corpse. The Governor and several gentlemen and officers and attendants came after.

This is memorable, that at such time as the King's body was brought out of St George's Hall; the sky was serene and clear, but presently it began to snow, and fell so fast, as by that time they came to the West end of the Royal Chapel, the black velvet-pall was all white (the colour of innocency) being thick covered over with snow. So went the white King to his grave, in the 48th year of his age, and the 22nd year and 10th month of his reign.

*This was by the old style of reckoning.

APPENDICES

A. THE KING'S WRITTEN DEFENCE

From Rushworth's Collections

His Majesty still persisting not to own the Court, they refused to permit him to deliver his reasons against the jurisdiction of the Court by word of mouth. Nevertheless his Majesty thought fit to leave them in writing to posterity, which follow in these words.

'Having already made my protestations, not only against the illegality of this pretended Court, but also, that no earthly power can justly call me (who am your King) in question as a delinquent, I would not any more open my mouth upon this occasion, more than to refer myself to what I have spoken, were I in this case alone concerned. But the duty I owe to God in the preservation of the true liberty of my people will not suffer me at this time to be silent. For how can any free-born subject of England call life or anything he possesseth his own, if power without right daily make new and abrogate the old fundamental laws of the land. Which I now take to be the present case. Wherefore when I came hither, I expected that you would have endeavoured to have satisfied me concerning these grounds, which hinder me to answer to your pretended impeachment. But since I see that nothing I can say will move you to it (the negatives are not so naturally proved as affirmatives) yet I will show you the reason why I am confident you cannot judge me, nor indeed the meanest man in England. For I will not (like you) without showing a reason, seek to impose a belief upon my subjects.

'There is no proceeding just against any man, but what is warranted either by God's Laws, or the municipal laws of the Country where he lives. Now I am most confident this day's proceeding cannot be warranted by God's laws. For on the contrary, the authority of obedience unto Kings is clearly warranted, and strictly commanded in both the Old and New Testament, which if denied, I am ready instantly to prove.

'And for the question now in hand, there it is said, that "where the word of a King is, there is power, and who may say unto him, 'what dost thou' " (Eccles. VIII. 4). Then for the law of this Land, I am no less confident that no learned Lawyer will affirm that an impeachment can lie against the King, they all going in his name. And one of their maxims is, that the King can do no wrong. Besides, the law upon which you ground your proceedings, must either be old or new; if old, show it, if new, tell what authority, warranted by the fundamental laws of the land, hath made it, and when. But how the House of Commons can erect a Court of Judicature, which was never one itself (as is well known to all lawyers) I leave to God and the World to judge. And it were full as strange, that they should pretend to make laws without the King or Lords House, to any that have heard speak of the Laws of England.

'And admitting, but not granting, that the people of England's Commission could grant your pretended power, I see nothing you can show for that, for certainly you never asked the question of the tenth man in the Kingdom, and in this way you manifestly wrong even the poorest ploughman, if you demand not his free consent. Nor can you pretend any colour for this your pretended commission, without the consent at least of the major part of every man in England of whatsoever quality or condition, which I am sure you never went about to seek, so far are you from having it. Thus you see that

THE EXECUTION

I speak not for my own right alone, as I am your King, but also for the true liberty of all my subjects, which consists not in the power of Government, but in living under such Laws, such a Government, as may give themselves the best assurance of their lives, and property of their Goods. Nor in this must or do I forget the privileges of both Houses of Parliament, which this day's proceedings do not only violate, but likewise occasion the greatest breach of their public faith that (I believe) ever was heard of, with which I am far from charging the two Houses, for all the pretended Crimes laid against me bear date long before this treaty at Newport. In which I, having concluded as much as in me lay and hopefully expecting the Houses Agreement thereunto, was suddenly surprised and hurried from thence as a prisoner, upon which account I am against my will brought hither. Where, since I am come, I cannot but to my power defend the ancient Laws and Liberties of this Kingdom, together with my own just right. Then for anything I can see, the higher House is totally excluded, and for the House of Commons, it is too well known that the major part of them are detained or deterred from sitting, so as if I had no other, this were sufficient for me to protest against the lawfulness of your pretended Court. Besides all this, the peace of the Kingdom is not the least in my thoughts, and what hope of settlement is there, so long as power reigns without rule or law, changing the whole form of that Government, under which this Kingdom hath flourished for many hundred years (nor will I say what will fall out in case this lawless, unjust proceeding against me do go on) and believe it, the Commons of England will not thank you for this Change, for they will remember how happy they have been of late years under the Reigns of Queen Elizabeth, the King my Father, and myself, until the beginning of these unhappy troubles, and will have cause to doubt, that they shall never be so happy under any new. And by this time it will be too sensibly evident, that the arms I took up, were only to defend the fundamental laws of this Kingdom against those who have supposed my power hath totally changed the ancient Government.

'Thus having showed you briefly the reasons why I cannot submit to your pretended authority, without violating the trust which I have from God for the welfare and liberty of my people, I expect from you either clear reasons to convince my judgment, showing me that I am in an error (and then truly I will answer) or that you will withdraw you proceedings.

'This I intended to speak in Westminster Hall on Monday January 22, but against reason was hindered to show my reasons.'

B. EXTRACT FROM THE
NARRATIVE OF JOHN DOWNES

From 'A True and Humble Representation of John Downes Esq., touching the Death of the Late King, so far as he may be concerned therein.'
[*Printed, after the Restoration, when Downes was about to stand trial as a regicide. He was condemned but afterwards reprieved and kept a close prisoner in Newgate and, later, in the Tower. He was still imprisoned in* 1666].

. . . 'When the Court was sate, and the King brought, the President told him that he had been charged with Treason, Perjury, Murder and other high Crimes committed against the People of this Nation, and that he had refused to give an answer to the Charge, demurring to the Jurisdiction of the Court; that he had been told the Court was satisfied of their own Jurisdiction, and that He was not to be the Judge of it; and that He had had several dayes given him for consideration; and that this was the last day the Court would demand of Him, whether He would answer to the Charge or not; if not, the Court would take the whole Charge, *Pro Confesso*, and would proceed to Judgement; (or words to this effect). The King (with such undaunted composedness and wisdom as I never beheld in man) made answer to this effect, that He could not acknowledge the Jurisdiction of the Court. He acknowledged they had power enough indeed, "but where is your authority? Yet", said He, "because I see you are ready to give a Sentence, and that such a Sentence may sooner be repented of than revoked, and that the peace of the Nation may so much depend upon it, I think fit to let you know that I desire to speak with my Parliament, for I have something to offer unto them which will be satisfactory to you all, and will be for the present Settlement of the Nation." The President regarded not these gracious expressions, but told Him he could take no notice of anything He said, save only to demand once again whether He would answer to his Charge or not.

'Then the King, not in passion, but with the greatest earnestness of affection, desired the Court that they would once more consider of it; "For" said He, "you may live to repent of such a Sentence," and therefore desired they would withdraw but for half an hour. "Or", said He, "if that be too much trouble for you, I will withdraw" (and passionately moved his body).

'The President was not affected with all this, but commanded the Clerk to read the Sentence. God knows I lie not, my heart was ready to burst within me. And as it fell out, sitting on the seat next to Cromwell, he perceived some discomposure in me, and turned to me and said, "What ails thee? Art thou mad? Canst thou not sit still and be quiet?" I answered "Quiet! No Sir, I cannot be quiet", and then presently I stood up, and with an audible voice said: "My Lord President, I am not satisfied to give my consent to this Sentence, but have reasons to offer to you against it, and therefore I desire the Court may adjourn to hear me." Then the President stood up and said "Nay, if any Member of the Court be unsatisfied, then the Court must adjourn." And accordingly they did adjourn into the inner Court of Wards.

'When the Court was sate there (all but Members and some officers being turned out) I was called by Cromwell to give an Account why I had put this trouble and disturbance upon the Court? I answered, (and so near as possibly I can, after so great an elapse of time, I will set down my very Syllabical expressions): "My Lord President, I should have been very glad that his Majesty would have condescended to these expressions long before this time—I say I should have been glad of it, both for His own sake and for ours. But sir, to me they are not too late, but welcome now, for sir, God knows I desire not the King's Death, but his Life. All that I thirst after is the Settlement of the Nation in peace. His Majesty now doth offer it, and, in order to it, desires to speak with his Parliament. Should you give Sentence of Death upon Him, before you have acquainted the Parliament with His offers, in my humble opinion, your case will be much altered, and you will do the greatest Action upon the greatest disadvantage imaginable, and I know not however you will be able to answer it."

'Cromwell, in some scornful wrath, stood up and answered me, (so near as I can remember in these words): "My Lord President, you see what weighty Reasons this Gentleman hath produced, that should move him to put this trouble upon you. Surely this Gentleman doth know he hath to deal with the hardest-hearted man upon the earth. However, Sir, it is not the single opinion of one peevish tenacious man that must sway the Court; nor defer them from their duty in so great a business. And I wish his Conscience doth not tell him (what ever he pretends of dissatisfaction) that he only would save his old Master. Therefore Sir, I pray you, lose no more time, but return to the Court and do your Duty."

'Not one soul would second me, nor speak one word, yet I knew divers by name. Sir John Bourcher, Mr Dixwell, Mr Love, Mr Waite, and some others were much unsatisfied, yet durst not speak. But on the contrary, divers Members took their turns with me in private discourse. Cromwell himself whispered me in the ear and said, by this and Mr Fry's business he was satisfied;* I arrived at nothing but making a mutiny in the Army, and cutting of throats. Another told me the Generations to come would have cause to curse my actings. And another (which sunk deepest of all) told me, that if I were in my wits I would never have done this, seeing I was before (as indeed I was) acquainted that the King, to save his life, would make these offers, but it would be as much as my life were worth to make any Disturbance. "And besides," said he, "it is not in the power of man, nor of this Parliament, to save his life. For the whole Army are resolved that if there be but any check or demur in giving Judgement, they will immediately fall upon him and hew him to pieces, and the House itself will not be out of Danger."

'To those whose height would permit me to speak and make replies, I told them to me it was evident the Parliament expected some such offers from the King. Why else did they make that order, that upon any emergency which could not be thought of, that the Court should immediately acquaint the House therewith: and there was such an order entered and to be seen in the Books, if he who in appearance ordered all matters hath not torn that order out, as I have heard he

---

*John Fry (1609–57), a theological writer and Member of Parliament for Shaftesbury, was included in the commission for the King's trial, though he only attended the early sittings of the court, and did not sign the death warrant.

On 15th January 1649 Downes accused him of blasphemy for denying the deity of Christ, and a few days later they were involved in argument in the Painted Chamber, where the court was about to sit. Downes proposed bringing a formal charge against Fry, and the latter was suspended from the Commons until he had cleared himself by a written definition of his position.

Cromwell may have thought this part of a more general plan to discredit the King's judges and provoke disagreement among them.

hath done all the rest of the proceedings. And inferred what greater emergencies could be than that the King demurred to the jurisdiction of the Court, and yet desired to speak with the Parliament, and offered to do that which would be satisfaction to all, especially seeing (as was pretended) that his denying to do such things was the ground which forced such a proceeding with him. And so without any more debate they returned to the Court, and I left them and went into the Speaker's Chamber, and there with tears eased my heart. . . . Nor did I ever give them one meeting more, but wholly from that time deserted them, though I was often summoned to meet them in the Painted Chamber. . . .

. . . 'And as this relation shows, I am but a weak, imprudent man, yet I did what I could. I did my best, I could do no more. I was single, I was alone; only I ought not to have been there at all.'

C. THE DEATH WARRANT OF CHARLES I

THE original warrant, 18 in. wide and 10 in. deep, is now preserved in the Library of the House of Lords. It was given to Colonel Hacker as his authority for carrying out the execution, and remained in his possession until his trial in 1660, when it was handed over to the Crown. It reads as follows:

At the high Court of Justice for the tryinge and iudginge of Charles Steuart Kinge of England January xxixth Anno Dñi 1648. Whereas Charles Steuart Kinge of England is and standeth convicted attaynted and condemned of High Treason and other high Crymes, And sentence uppon Saturday last/^{was} pronounced against him by this Court to be putt to death by the severinge of his head from his body Of wch sentence execučon yet remayneth to be done, These are therefore to will and require you to see the said sentence executed In the open Streete before Whitehall uppon the morrowe being the Thirtieth day of this instante moneth of January betweene the houres of Tenn in the morninge and Five in the afternoone of the same day wth full effect And for soe doing this shall be yor sufficient warrant And these are to require All Officers and Souldiers and other the good people of this Nation of England to be assistinge unto you in this Service

Given under our hands and Seales

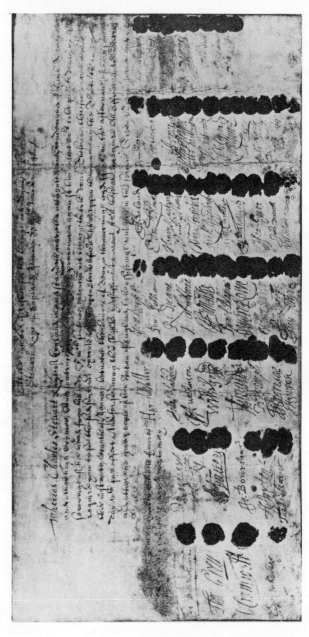

THE DEATH WARRANT

To Colonell Ffrancis Hacker, Colonell Huncks and Lieutenant Colonell Phayre and to every of them

Jo. Bradshawe	Ri.Deane	Tho.Horton
Tho. Grey	Robert Tichborne	J. Jones
O. Cromwell	H. Edwardes	John Moore
Edw. Whalley	Daniel Blagraue	Gilbt. Millington
M. Liuesey	Owen Rowe	G. Fleetwood
John Okey	William Purefoy	J. Alured
J. Dauers	Ad. Scrope	Robt. Lilburne
Jo. Bourchier	James Temple	Will. Say
H. Ireton	A. Garland	Anth. Stapley
Tho. Mauleuerer	Edm. Ludlowe	Greg. Norton
Har. Waller	Henry Marten	Tho. Challoner
John Blakiston	Vinct. Potter	Tho. Wogan
J. Hutchinson	Wm. Constable	John Venn
Willi. Goff	Rich. Ingoldesby	Gregory Clement
Tho. Pride	Willi. Cawley	Jo. Downes
Pe. Temple	Jo. Barkestead	Tho. Wayte
T. Harrison	Isaa. Ewer	Tho. Scot
J. Hewson	John Dixwell	Jo. Carew
Hen. Smyth	Valentine Wanton	Miles Corbet
Per. Pelham	Symon Mayne	

The words underlined have been written over erasures and this has given rise to speculation about the original date of the warrant, since 'xxixth' in the second line is a later addition, and the word 'Thirtieth' has been spread out to fill a wide space that had been left for it. Most striking of all is the date of sentence, inserted over an erasure which leaves too little space for it, so that the word 'was' has been interlined. The most convincing hypothesis is that the warrant was originally drawn up on the 25th, and dated for the following day, when it was intended to sentence the King in his absence, but that some of the judges insisted that the King should be given one more opportunity to accept the jurisdiction of the court. The warrant was therefore set aside, though some judges had apparently already signed it, and modifications were made after the King had finally been sentenced on the 27th.

A simpler solution would have been a new warrant, but this would have meant obtaining signatures a second time from those who had already signed, and it seems that by the 29th some, at least, might have changed their minds. Cromwell and a small group of determined men had to put great pressure on the judges to extort sufficient signatures. In the end, out of the sixty-seven members of the court who had been present when the King was sentenced, fifty-eight signed their names—the other signature was that of Ingoldesby, who had not actually been present in court on that day. According to Clarendon, Cromwell held Ingoldesby's hand and forced him to write, but the firmness of his signature would seem to disprove this. No doubt Cromwell used every means of persuasion, including threats, and Downes's account in Appendix B shows how frightening he could be; but in fact the nine who refused to sign came to no harm.

D. HERBERT'S DREAM

IN a letter of 1680 he wrote:
. . . .'The King, some hours before day, drew his bed curtain to awaken me, and could by the light of the wax-lamp perceive me troubled in my sleep. The King rose forthwith; and as I was making him ready, "Herbert", said the King, "I would know why you were disquieted in your sleep?" I replied: "May it please your Majesty, I was in a dream." "What was your dream?", said the King, "I would hear it." "May it please your Majesty," said I, "I dreamed, that as you were making ready, one knocked at the bed-chamber door, which your Majesty took no notice of, nor was I willing to acquaint you with it, apprehending it might be Colonel Hacker. But knocking the second time, your Majesty asked me, if I heard it not? I said I did; but did not use to go without his order. 'Why then, go; know who it is and his business.' Whereupon I opened the door, and perceived that it was the Lord Archbishop of Canterbury, Dr Laud,* in his Pontifical Habit, as worn at Court; I knew him, having seen him often. The Archbishop desired he might enter, having something to say to the King. I acquainted your Majesty with his desire; so you bad me let him in. Being in, he made his obeisance to your Majesty in the middle of the room, do-ing the like also when he came near your person; and, falling on his knees, your Majesty gave him your hand to kiss, and took him aside to the window, where some discourse passed

*Executed January 10, 1645.

between your Majesty and him, and I kept a becoming distance, not hearing anything that was said, yet could perceive your Majesty pensive by your looks, and that the Archbishop gave a sign; who, after a short stay, again kissing your hand, returned, but with face all the way towards your Majesty, and making his usual reverences, the third being so submiss, as he fell prostrate on his face on the ground, and I immediately stept to him to help him up, which I was then acting, when your Majesty saw me troubled in my sleep. The impression was so lively, that I looked about, verily thinking it was no dream."

'The King said, my dream was remarkable, "but he is dead; yet, had we conferred together during life, 'tis very likely (albeit I love him well) I should have said something to him might have occasioned his sign." '

INDEX